MW01104339

FAITH
takes
ACTION

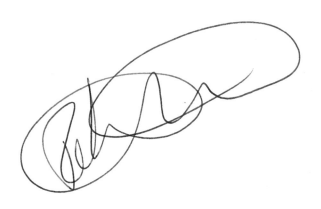

FAITH
takes
ACTION

REBECCA
MURZIN

TATE PUBLISHING & *Enterprises*

Published by Tate Publishing & Enterprises, LLC
127 E. Trade Center Terrace | Mustang, Oklahoma 73064 USA
1.888.361.9473 | www.tatepublishing.com

Tate Publishing is committed to excellence in the publishing industry. The company reflects the philosophy established by the founders, based on Psalm 68:11,
"The Lord gave the word and great was the company of those who published it."

Book design copyright © 2010 by Tate Publishing, LLC. All rights reserved.
Cover design by Lindsay B. Behrens
Interior design by Chris Webb

Published in the United States of America

ISBN: 978-1-61663-555-8
1. Religion / Christian Life / Spiritual Growth
2. Religion / Biblical Commentary / General
10.05.11

DEDICATION

I dedicate this book first and foremost to God: to the Father, who created all and gave each of us our talents; to His Son, Jesus Christ, who died for our sins and made salvation for us possible; to the Holy Spirit, who, with the leading and guidance, prompted me to write this book and gives me constant direction for my life.

Then I dedicate it to all my brothers and sisters in Christ who diligently seek the Lord and continue to improve their walk with the Lord and seek to follow His will.

Acknowledgments

I would like to thank my wonderful husband, Donnie. He has supported me in everything the Lord leads me to do. He is a huge encouragement and is in constant prayer for the direction and steps we should take. His faith has been unmovable during this entire process.

I would also like to thank Evan, Naomi, and Joseph, my three loving children. They have shown excitement and encouragement ever since I began this book. They have truly manifested the fruits of the spirit. Many times I have been at the computer, and they lovingly wait until I stop to ask for things.

TABLE OF CONTENTS

FOREWORD

This book by Rebecca Murzin is essential to all believers. For new believers, it helps to learn to be obedient to God. It has real examples of what life can do and how God, through His Word, can direct, heal, and use us. This book shows us how to take action through the questions, through the scriptures, and through faith.

For mature believers, it is an excellent guide. It helps us to examine ourselves; it helps us to focus on God and His Word. It helps us to know how to dig in deeper. We all need to become stronger in the kingdom of God and less in the world's kingdom.

This book is truly inspired by the Holy Spirit. It is thoughtful, concise, and straightforward. It is to be used by all, either on our own or even in Bible studies, as we need to take action to use God's Word effectively and practically. Praise God that Rebecca is able to make this book down to earth and so useful for the body of Christ. I look forward to the Holy Spirit using Rebecca again for the next books and will treasure and use this book now as I walk my path in Christ Jesus.

This book, I believe, is a launch pad to an incredible life that God has for you and your family. I read *Faith Takes Action* in only three days. What was even more exciting is that I am not a reader of many books, only my Bible. I meditated on every word written. If we are listening to God, He has said these things to every believer. I know, because he has spoken many of these things to my heart, bringing me also to repentance through this book. I also believe this book delivers a timely message to us right now. I could go on, but I will not. Just read this book for yourselves and be blessed with its content. Amen!

Brother and sister in Christ Jesus,

—Reverend George E. Reese Jr.
and Mrs. Karen Lee Reese
Elder of Higher Ground Ministries, South Barnstead, New Hampshire Pastor, founder, and co-founder of Reese Family Ministries International, Epsom, New Hampshire

PROLOGUE

There is only one way to heaven and that is belief in the Lord Jesus Christ. We have all committed sin, and praise God He sent his Son to die for them and wash them away by his precious blood. He willingly forgives us and welcomes us into his kingdom. We are going to take a look at what that truly means and how to walk it out. Belief in Jesus begins with a confession of the mouth, but that is not the extent of it. To believe in the Lord means to follow him and be obedient to his Word. Both the Old and New Testament of the Bible show us this. If we love God and truly in our hearts believe in Him, we will obey Him and do all that he has commanded. We are his servants, and he commands us; we do not command Him. He does not bend at our whim or conform to our ideas of how things should be done. God is the same yesterday, today, and forever. There is only one true way to know what God wants and desires for us and that is to have an intimate relationship with him. God desires this for us. He wants to be our friend and says we are if we do what he has commanded (John 14:15). When you are intimate with someone, you talk and listen to the other person. You search him or her out and find out what he or she likes and dislikes. This is how our relationship with the Lord should be. We can get there by reading his Word, spending time in prayer, and listening to and for his voice.

If you have never asked the Lord to be your Savior or have but never followed through with your commitment (begun to walk away from your old ways and begun to take up the Lord's), I would like to invite you now to do so. Whether it's for the first time or making a fresh start and recommitment, you can confess this and pray that the Lord would come in and do a new work in you.

Father, I thank you for sending your Son, Jesus Christ to die on the cross for me and washing away my sin. I believe that Jesus is the Son of God, born of the Virgin Mary, and that He died and rose again on the third day, is alive, and is sitting now at the right hand of God. I believe that the Bible is the inspired Word of God. I choose to follow all of it and not only the parts that are easy. I choose to obey the Lord and his word. I ask that the Holy Spirit would come into me now and fill me that I might be able to be led and walk in the power and authority that the Lord has given me through Jesus.

Many Christians today haven't fallen away from the Word of God. Many do not read the Bible for themselves. They simply rely on what others tell them the Bible says or what they hear preached on Sunday. This leaves them on shaky ground. Their faith is not rooted and can easily be ripped up. Others are reading the Word, yet they are only receiving the happy parts or the things they can manage to follow because it fits into their lifestyle. How can we know God's will if we don't search it out, study it, and meditate upon it? They have begun to believe and preach a false doctrine. We need to be searching out and only preaching the truth. We are truly all special to Him. He knows us all intimately and desires that we seek to know Him in this way as well. I pray this book inspires you to become all that you were created to be and helps you to fulfill the purpose and calling the Lord has for you. None of us is perfect, but we can spend our lives continually striving to reach the goal of doing all that He asks of us with complete and joyful obedience.

The faith in action questions at the end of each chapter are there to help you take an honest look at your life and walk. They are not meant to bring false condemnation but to help you get on track and fix things that you might not have otherwise seen in your life. We all have things we need to change and get rid of. That is part of our walk. With the grace of God, we can do it. If you need more room than the lines provided for, that's okay; you can get more paper. You are not restricted to this book.

WHAT IS JOHN 3:16 REALLY SAYING?

We as Christians need to stop thinking we can write a script to heaven. We take John 3:16 and run with it. We have come up with a packaged prayer for people and believe that is all we need to do and say. Many Christians, including myself, until recently, when the leading of the Spirit led me to investigate deeper, have wanted to lead others to the Lord and grow our churches so much that we have led to telling people a half truth just to get them in. We are telling people a half truth by telling people part of the truth or only a very small portion of what is required to receive salvation and all that the Lord has for them and is required from them. We are deceiving these people, and they might never actually go to heaven. They will not make it because they were told all they had to do was say this simple prayer and they were in. This is not the truth; it is only half of what is required and essentially a lie. When we don't tell the whole truth it is the same as telling a lie. Partial truth misrepresents. We must devote our lives to the Lord and walk out our salvation with fear and trembling so that our names are not blotted out of the book of life. Professing that the Lord is Savior is important and required, yet it needs to truly be believed from the heart, and when it is, our lives will show it. The problem is that these people believe what they have heard to be everything they need to know. They don't investigate the Word or read the Bible for themselves. They occasionally go to church and may or may not believe what they hear in church on Sunday. They continue on with their lives as it always has been, only thinking now they have added a new meeting in their schedules with the born-again club. The Bible warns against doing this. In James 1:22, it says, "But be ye doers of the word, and not hearers only, deceiving your own selves." Since we see them attending on occasion or even regularly, we think to ourselves, *Well done*. We go on to other things, never disciplining them further because now they have joined our club so everything must be fine and dandy. The sad thing is we have done this so long and only told people the half of it for so long that we have begun to believe the lie ourselves. I believe that the mass deception of salvation has saddened the Lord. Let's look at John 3:16 and see what it really says.

> For God so loved the world, that he gave his only begotten Son, that whosoever believeth in him should not perish, but have everlasting life.
>
> John 3:16

The Crossmap Dictionary defines *believe* as "To have a firm persuasion of any thing, 2. To expect or hope with confidence; to trust. To believe in, is to hold as the object of faith." The Greek word for believe is *pisteuo* and is translated "to have faith." So far, we see that we could say it like this: For God so loved the world, that he gave his only begotten son, that whosoever has a firm persuasion of faith in him shall not perish, but have everlasting life." When something is firm, it is not easily moved. We need a strong, unshakeable foundation in our faith that can't be easily changed by what others say or do. We need God's Word and Holy Spirit so ingrained in our hearts that when an untruth is spoken, it will instantly put a check in our spirit or heart. We can't even be swayed by our emotions and anger. It is especially important to not be swayed by the tempting thoughts put into our minds by Satan. You can be sure the devil wants us to think that there is nothing we can do about it. Wow, does he get mad when we discover the truth and begin to apply it. We are able to take each thought captive and cast out imaginations.

> For though we walk in the flesh, we do not war after the flesh: For the weapons of our warfare are not carnal, but mighty through God to the pulling down of strong holds Casting down imaginations, and every high thing that exalteth itself against the knowledge of God, and bringing into captivity every thought to the obedience of Christ.
>
> 2 Corinthians 10:3–5

In this scripture we can see that God is telling us one way to be firm is to remember we are not only fighting a physical battle of everyday life but a spiritual battle as well; this battle often takes place in our minds. Yet the awesome thing is he goes on to tell us that he has given us the power to win and describes the battle plan. Take control of your mind! Be aware of each thought that enters in and ask yourself, *Should I meditate on this further or does it exalt itself against (the opposite of) the Word of God?* If it does, capture it. Do not meditate or think about it any further. Make the conscious choice to cast the thought out of your mind and choose to think on the truth, which are the things of God. We are not ill equipped. God has shown us another important thing we can do to be firm and unmoved in our faith and the attacks in life.

> Finally, my brethren, be strong in the Lord, and in the power of his might. Put on the whole armour of God, that ye may be able to stand against the wiles of the devil. For we wrestle not against flesh and blood, but against principalities, against powers, against the rulers of the darkness of this world, against spiritual wickedness in high places. Wherefore take unto you the whole armour of God, that ye may be able to withstand in the evil day, and having done all, to stand. Stand therefore, having your loins girt about with truth, and having on the breastplate of righteousness; And your feet shod with the preparation of the gospel of peace; Above all, taking the shield of faith, wherewith ye shall be able to quench all the fiery darts of the wicked. And take the helmet of salvation, and the sword of the Spirit, which is the word of God: Praying always with all prayer and supplication in the Spirit, and watching thereunto with all perseverance and supplication for all saints; And for me, that utterance may be given unto me, that I may open my mouth boldly, to make known the mystery of the gospel, For which I am an ambassador in bonds: that therein I may speak boldly, as I ought to speak.
>
> Ephesians 6:10–20

When we put on the armor of God, it allows us to have that divine protection. This will help you to stand firm. I love Paul's prayer at the end that he may open his mouth boldly to make known the mystery of the gospel. That is also my prayer for you as you read and study this book, that God would give you the boldness, authority, and strength to go make known the gospel and the mysteries in it to all those around you, in your workplaces, in your homes, towns, supermarkets, wherever you might encounter those who do not know Jesus, and all over the world. I pray that you be sensitive to the leading of the Holy Spirit to step out and minister to whomever the Lord leads you to and opens the doors for you in spreading his gospel.

Let's go back to believe meaning "to have a firm persuasion of any thing, 2. to expect or hope with confidence; to trust." It is translated literally as "to have faith." The King James Dictionary defines *faith* as "belief, or the object of belief." So we can clearly see here that faith and believe can be used interchangeably. Let's use the best source we have to fully describe what faith (belief) is. Hebrews 11:1 defines faith: "Now faith is the substance *(realization)* of things hoped for, the evidence *(conviction)* of things not seen." I italicized the footnotes from the Bible in parentheses. I want us to look at the word *hope*. The International Bible Dictionary says under the word *hope* "devotion to Christ produced a religious experience that gave certainty to hope." The Strong's Greek Dictionary gives the Greek word *elpizo* for the phrase "of things hoped for" and defines it as "to expect or confide." When we are expecting something, we are actively waiting. This is exactly what we do when we believe in Jesus; we actively wait for him to give us direction for our life. We also have a relationship with Him; we confide in Him through prayer. Relationships take work. We can't have a relationship with anyone including God if we don't take an active role. Relationships are two-way. We confide in God then we expect and wait for Him to respond.

Most people say that if you go to church and or believe in God, you are religious. About six out of ten times that I mention anything to do with God, the Bible, or church in front of someone I don't know his or her initial response is, "You must be religious" or "Are you religious?" I used to say, "No, I just believe in what the Bible says." I related religion to manmade traditions because I did not understand the true meaning of *religious*. Now I am proud to say that I am religious. We have already learned that hope is related to being religious. If this alone isn't enough, see what the definition of religious is. The International Standard Bible Encyclopedia defines *religious* as "used frequently to denote the outward expression of worship." Note that *worship* is a verb and therefore an action word. Outward implies more than just something you feel on the inside. The Encyclopedia Britannica Dictionary (EBD) defines *religious* as "relating to or manifesting faithful devotion to an acknowledged ultimate reality or deity. The word *manifest* really stands out to me; it is also a verb. The International Bible Encyclopedia states that the word *manifest* means "to make apparent." That is exactly what God wants us to do in Matthew 5:16. The Bible tells us, "Let your light so shine before men, that they may see your good works, and glorify your Father which is in heaven." A light in a dark place is very apparent. There is absolutely no denying that the light is there. Our lives should be a constant reminder to all those in the dark that Jesus is there and is absolutely real. We should always have an outward expression of worship to our Lord. In 2 Corinthians 4:5–6, it states, "For we preach not ourselves, but Christ Jesus the Lord; and ourselves your servants for Jesus' sake. For God, who commanded the light to shine out of the darkness, hath shined in our hearts, to give the light of the knowledge of the glory of God in the face of Jesus Christ."

We can see now that believing is not a confession with the mouth only but an action. Essentially, it is a change in our lifestyle. We outwardly express our worship of God by doing things He tells us to do: loving our neighbor, tithing, obeying authority, giving him praise, and so on. It becomes a progression of letting go of our old ways (old man) and taking up God's ways (new man) as God reveals things to us. This is made clear in 2 Corinthians 5:17: "Therefore if any man be in Christ, he is a new creature: old things are passed away: behold all things are become new."

Think about it in this way: when you really believe in something, you take action. It also takes action for you to acknowledge someone else's belief in something. For example, if someone came up to you and said that he believed it was important to take care of the environment, yet his life proved otherwise by his actions, would you believe him? If the person who said it to you was constantly heaping up huge piles of garbage to go off to the landfill, always had a new plastic bottle of bottled water, and used aerosol hairspray every day and never recycled or reused, would you believe he meant what he said? Of course not. Now, a second person came up to you and said the same thing. As you observed this person, you noticed she always carried a plastic bottle of water that she refilled herself, used cloth bags at the grocery store, recycled all she could and had very little waste, and encouraged others to do the same. Would you believe this second person meant what she said?

Yes, you would know it because her lifestyle proved it, just as God will know you believe in Jesus because your lifestyle will prove it.

God gave us a free will. Therefore, we need to prove we believe what is right. If saying something was enough for God, then Adam and Eve would have never been kicked out of the garden. The Israelites would never have had to wander around the desert for forty years. If saying something was enough and it was all that was required, then our precious and most wonderful Savior never would have had to endure the agonizing pain of being nailed to that cross. Jesus would have just said, "Father, take these children as your own. I love them and am willing to take their sins onto myself, so that you will redeem them, forgive them, and blot out their sins forever." Wouldn't that be wonderful? God the Father's Son, Jesus, would never have had to suffer, be tortured, and be put through the most humiliating and agonizing death. Yet he did because he needed to prove by his actions that he felt that way. In this the Father also proved by his actions how much he loved us. How many of us could do for God what he has done for us? Not one, which is why we dedicate our life in service and sacrifice to him. It is essential that we are constantly reaffirming our love and appreciation for Him.

When you truly believe in something, a cause, or a person, you take action. You will follow after it, and it will become a way of life. It will be second nature. When we believe in Jesus, we will do what he tells us to do. Jesus says, "You are my friend if you do whatever I command you" (John 15:14).

So we see Jesus saying that we must take action. We need to do what he has commanded us to do. We find out what he has commanded by reading his Word.

The Bible makes it very clear that he is the author of salvation to those who obey. "And being made perfect, he became the author of eternal salvation unto all them that obey him" (Hebrews 5:9).

Again, there must be action. You can't truly believe in something and not move on it; believing is doing. We must obey! When we choose to accept Jesus as our Lord and Savior, we are to relinquish our will and take up God's. Jesus tells us this when He tells us how to pray. Here is an excerpt from the Lord's Prayer: "Thy kingdom come. Thy will be done in earth, as it is in heaven" (Mathew 6:10).

It was not about Jesus's will; it was about the Father's! Jesus spoke his heart to his Father in the garden when He prayed, "Father, If thou be willing, remove this cup from me: nevertheless not my will, But thine, be done" (Luke 22:42).

Then Jesus followed through with his actions and proving his faith, allowing himself to be taken and crucified. Again, the Bible shows us that even Jesus had to prove to God through actions. Look at what Jesus says to God the Father:

> These words spake Jesus, and lifted up his eyes to heaven, and said, Father, the hour is come; glorify thy Son, that thy Son also may glorify thee: As thou hast given him power over all flesh, that he should give eternal life to as many as thou hast given him. And this is life eternal, that they might know thee the only true God, and Jesus Christ, whom thou hast sent. *I have* glorified thee on the earth: *I have* finished the work which thou gavest me to do. And now, O Father, glorify thou me with thine own self with the glory which I had with thee before the world was. *I have* manifested

thy name unto the men which thou gavest me out of the world: thine they were, and thou gavest them me; *and they have* kept thy word. Now *they have* known that all things whatsoever thou hast given me are of thee. *For I have* given unto them the words which thou gavest me; and *they have* received them, and have known surely that I came out from thee, and *they have* believed that thou didst send me.
John 17:1–8

I italicized the scripture above. The italics show us his actions, authority, and the reason for his coming. Then in verse 4 Jesus begins to remind God that salvation can happen and that He *proved* his love and belief by his *actions.* Jesus is telling God, "Look at my actions; I have done what you required." In verse 6 he also states, "I have manifested thy name." Remember that manifest means to make evident or certain by showing or displaying. So even Jesus had to show and remind the Father that He took action and showed others what God had given him to do. Jesus states, "They have kept thy word," reminding God of the disciples actions. Jesus said this so that the disciples would receive salvation.

We need to be extremely careful that we are not taking God's Word out of context just to get a "conversion." When we tell people only the partial truth, it is the same as a lie. We are accountable to God for what we tell others. If they don't understand the whole truth and just think they only have to say a prayer and can continue in their sinful life and go to heaven because of words they spoke years prior, it is a lie. We are responsible for that lie. If we truly love others with God's love (the only true love), then we will tell them the whole truth in love. Yes, we do need to confess Jesus and believe in him, but we need to explain that believing is a way of life and a change in lifestyle. The word *unbelief* in Greek is *apistia* and is translated to mean unfaithfulness (disobedience). If unbelief is disobedience, then I think it is safe to say (also we proved it previously) that belief is to obey. John 3:16 is a vital scripture to our faith. We need to really see and understand what God is saying and make sure we are telling others the full truth of what God is saying. We all want to see the world saved. That is a goal of every Christian and what Jesus has called us to do. But if our heart is to truly see them saved and not just to put another notch on our spiritual belt, then we need to make sure they are truly accepting Jesus and understand what it means to accept him. Spread the news, the good news that God sent his Son, Jesus, to forgive our sins. He died on the cross and was raised three days later and is now in heaven sitting at the right hand of God. It is time to step out in faith and begin telling people the whole truth of what believing in God really is. It is first a confession followed by actions that prove what you say. We prove our belief in Jesus by manifesting obedience to His Word. So go and tell the world that God gave His Son, and if we believe in him—truly believe (not just saying a prayer and continuing on with life as always)—we are in Christ and new creatures and we will not perish but have an everlasting life that will be with God Almighty. Life starts now as we continue in an everlasting relationship of growing, learning, obeying, and worshiping the creator.

> Jesus, I recognize you as our Lord and Savior. Please help me to live a life that honors you and shows my true faith and who you are to all those around me. Let my light so shine that others will

be drawn to you. Help me to speak and live your
Word in truth and love. Lord, I choose to lay my
plans for my life and the way I think I should
live down. I choose now to take up your plan and
way. Please help me to walk out my faith and the
awesome and mighty plan that you have for my
life. Thank you, Lord, for all that you have done
for me and all that you have planned for me. I
love you, God, and give you all the honor and
glory. Amen.

You may want to write down notes on chapter and
thoughts responding to prayer such as proclaiming the
things He has done for you.

_____

_____

_____

_____

FAITH IN ACTION QUESTIONS

1. What stood out to me the most in this chapter?

_____

_____

2. Am I living a life that proves my belief in Jesus?

_____

3. In what ways do I prove it?

_____

_____

_____

_____

4. What actions in my life do not line up with my beliefs?

_____

_____

_____

_____

5. Who is around me that I can share Jesus with?

_____

_____

FAITH WITHOUT WORKS IS DEAD

We have all heard from the pulpit many times that we are not saved by works but faith! We as Christians know this to be true from everything inside us. We worship and exalt our King for this very reason. We praise his name for his mercy that has washed away our sins. His grace and mercy are truly the only reasons we are going to that beautiful place that no human could ever fully describe; we're only given a vague glimpse of what he has prepared for us. There is certainly no good work that can get us there alone. Faith in him is a must. The thing is we have neglected to acknowledge is that true faith in him drives us to serve him, love others, and to do the works he has called us to do.

Of course, we know that anything he calls us to do is a good work because God is good! So true faith leads and can't be without good works ordained by God. The book of James makes this very clear. Without faith in Jesus, you go to hell. Without works, you don't have faith. Therefore, you are not saved by works but faith. Although you can't have faith without works. At first this might sound a little confusing, but let's look at the Word of God, pull it apart, and begin to make sense of it.

Believing that Jesus is the Son of God and our Savior is necessary for salvation and is definitely the very first step on the path of serving the Most High, but it is not enough. If all that occurs is a verbal statement and nothing else happens in the heart, there is no guarantee of salvation.

> What doth it profit, my brethren, though a man say he hath faith, and have not works? Can faith save him? If a brother or sister be naked, and destitute of daily food, And one of you say unto them, Depart in peace, be ye warmed and filled; notwithstanding ye give them not those things which are needful to the body; what doth it profit? Even so faith, if it hath not works, is dead, being alone. Yea, a man may say, Thou hast faith, and I have works: shew me thy faith without thy works, and I will shew thee my faith by my works. Thou believest that there is one God; thou doest well: the devils also believe, and tremble. But wilt thou know, O vain man, that faith without works is dead?
>
> James 2:14–20

What James is saying is that confessing you have faith alone and nothing more is not enough. Notice in this verse James states, "Though a man say he hath faith." This is making it clear that what comes out of his mouth is quite different from the truth. Saying one thing and doing another is hypocritical. Jesus states that hypocrites and those who begin to do evil will go to hell in Matthew 24:48–51: "But if that evil servant shall say in his heart, My lord delayeth his coming; and shall begin to smite his fellow servants, and to eat and drink with the drunken; The lord of that servant shall come in a day when he looketh not for him, and in an hour that he is not aware of, And shall cut him asunder, and appoint him a portion with the hypocrites: there shall be weeping and gnashing of teeth." In verse 14 James is asking, "What do you gain if you have faith and not works?" He is saying that if there are no good works, there is no true faith. Going on to verses 15–17, he is showing us that the love of God can't be in us if we see someone in need of the very things necessary for survival and do nothing about it. Demons even believe! Demons know Jesus is Lord. Yet they are still going to hell. Hell was made for them. They have chosen to do things contrary to the will and Word of God. Saying you believe has gained or profited nothing. Jesus commanded us to love our neighbors. Jesus also states:

> For I was an hungered, and ye gave me meat: I was thirsty, and ye gave me drink: I was a stranger, and ye took me in: Naked, and ye clothed me: I was sick, and ye visited me: I was in prison, and ye came unto me. Then shall the righteous answer him, saying, Lord, when saw we thee an hungered, and fed thee? or thirsty, and gave thee drink? When saw we thee a stranger, and took thee in? or naked, and clothed thee? Or when saw we thee sick, or in prison, and came unto thee? And the King shall answer and say unto them, Verily I say unto you, Inasmuch as ye have done it unto one of the least of these my brethren, ye have done it unto me. Then shall he say also unto them on the left hand, Depart from me, ye cursed, into everlasting fire, prepared for the devil and his angels: For I was an hungred, and ye gave me no meat: I was thirsty, and ye gave me no drink: I was a stranger, and ye took me

not in: naked, and ye clothed me not: sick, and in prison, and ye visited me not. Then shall they also answer him, saying, Lord, when saw we thee an hungred, or athirst, or a stranger, or naked, or sick, or in prison, and did not minister unto thee? Then shall he answer them, saying, Verily I say unto you, Inasmuch as ye did it not to one of the least of these, ye did it not to me. And these shall go away into everlasting punishment: but the righteous into life eternal.

Mathew 25:35–46

So we see that whatever we do to those around us, we are doing it unto the Lord. Demons and the devil believe and know that Jesus is the only true God. They acknowledge him, his authority, and power. We can see this in Matthew 8:29: "And, behold, they cried out, saying, What have we to do with thee, Jesus, thou Son of God? Art thou come hither to torment us before the time?"

We see again that the demons recognize Jesus to be the Son of God. They even know their outcome. They are defeated and know that he is able to torture them. Why we have believed Satan's lie and think they have the power to torture us, I don't know. Jesus has the power; they have none unless it is given to them. We can give it to them through unbelief, fear, and sin that we have chosen to continue walking in.

Abraham's belief was tested by God. Abraham proved his faith by his actions. He told God through his actions; I love you and trust your will over what I can understand. I believe that you are sovereign, and I lay my life and all that I have down to serve you (including the children given by you).

But wilt thou know, O vain man, that faith without works is dead? Was not Abraham our father justified by works, when he had offered Isaac his son upon the altar? Seest thou how faith wrought with his works, and by works was faith made perfect? And the scripture was fulfilled which saith, Abraham believed God, and it was imputed unto him for righteousness: and he was called the Friend of God. Ye see then how that by works a man is justified, and not by faith only. Likewise also was not Rahab the harlot justified by works, when she had received the messengers, and had sent them out another way? For as the body without the spirit is dead, so faith without works is dead also.

James 2:20–26

If we think that works are not needed, the Bible calls us vain. Let's see what the Strong's Greek and Hebrew Dictionary defines vain as: vain is *kenos* in Greek and is translated as "empty (literally or figuratively)." Well, that is about as plain as it gets. You are empty (or have nothing in you) if you don't know that faith without works is dead. If something is empty, it is worthless. When our jars in the refrigerator become empty, we throw them out because they are of no more use to us. They have become worthless and are taking up valuable space. Once something is empty, it can't be used. Therefore, it no longer has any relevance or significance. So if we are empty, we can have pride that is undue because there is nothing there. The awesome thing is when we have become empty (vain), we can always turn to our loving Savior full of grace, mercy, love, and forgiveness to fill us back up again. Praise God.

Abraham was called the friend of God because he

obeyed God. Jesus tells us that we can be his fiend also if we do the same thing. "Ye are my friends, if ye do whatsoever I command you" (John 15:14).

When we do as we are commanded, we are justified. The Greek word for *justified* is *dikaioo*. The translation for it is "to render (i.e., show or regard as) just or innocent." We by ourselves are not righteous or innocent, and what we say does not make us righteous. We have been made the righteousness of God through Christ Jesus (2 Corinthians 5:21). Through our belief in Jesus (following and obeying), we become righteous. When we believe in Jesus through our actions, we are justified, which is to regard as just or innocent.

In His Word, God has told us to correct or rebuke each other sharply for our actions. We should do this so that we would all be free from error in our faith. When we correct each other and share revelation, it enables us all to become stronger and have a more firm, unshakable faith. This allows us to withstand the attacks of the enemy and to be unburned in the fire. When we build the body with correction, we will not bend to the lies or fables told to us by the enemy. Satan can deceive us in many ways. He can use demons to whisper in our ear or use others and our fear of others to keep us believing his lies. The person being used by the devil to say something to you might not even know he or she is deceived. The person telling the lie could believe it himself, therefore making it all the more convincing. Every day people are unknowingly being used by the enemy. This is why it is so important to keep each other in check and not become offended with each other over constructive criticism. We are on the same side and are all fighting the same enemy. Let's get over ourselves and get down to the real business at hand: doing the will of the Father.

"This witness is true. Wherefore rebuke them sharply, that they may be sound in the faith; Not giving heed to Jewish fables, and commandments of men, that turn from the truth" (Titus 1:13–14).

When we are pure, all things that are of the Lord and truth are pure to us. Rebuke and correction are good, even if it does not feel good in the flesh for a brief moment. It might not feel good in our emotions for a time, but it will feel good and right in our spirit because it is ordained by the Lord. We will accept it. When we do not believe or accept it, we become defiled. "Unto the pure all things are pure: but unto them that are defiled and unbelieving is nothing pure; but even their mind and conscience is defiled" (Titus 1:15).

If we truly believe, love, and know that Jesus is Lord and Savior, then our actions and everything we do and say should prove it. When our actions do not line up with our words, we are denying Christ and have become hypocrites.

> If any man among you seem to be religious, and bridleth not his tongue, but deceiveth his own heart, this man's religion is vain. Pure religion and undefiled before God and the Father is this, To visit the fatherless and widows in their affliction, and to keep himself unspotted from the world.
>
> James 1:26–27

We need to be so careful to pay attention and stop ourselves from speaking damaging words. We see again here that our religion is in vain if we don't watch what we say. When we speak out things that do not line up with the Word of God, it can begin to sink into our hearts, and we will in turn deceive our own hearts. When we are deceived, then we are no longer doing the things that we need to be doing. James then goes on to say what true religion is. Every bit of it is action.

"They profess that they know God; but in works they deny him, being abominable, and disobedient, and unto every good work reprobate" (Titus 1:16). At the end of this verse, it lists what we are when we deny him in our works. The word *abominable* in Greek is *bdeluktos*. It means "detestable." When something is detestable, it is hated. So God is saying that when we deny him with our works, we are detestable and worthy of hatred. This is a very strong statement that makes me feel sick. Now we know that God does not hate us; he loves us. This verse shows us even more of how awesome his grace and mercy are. God states in black and white that we are truly worthy of hatred when our actions are contrary to his will. Praise God he loves us though we are not worthy. Even though he loves us, he will give us the consequence of our chosen action. "For we must all appear before the judgment seat of Christ; that every one may receive the things done in his body, according to that he hath done, whether it be good or bad' (2 Corinthians 5:10). The last part "and unto every good work reprobate" really got me thinking about the word *reprobate* and what it meant, so I looked it up. In the Greek, the word *reprobate* is *adokimos*. When reading in the International Standard Encyclopedia, it states that the first part of the word, *adoki* means "not acknowledged." It also says that the term "not genuine" can be simply attached to the word. Wettstien interpreted it as "an unfit mind," meaning unable to do normal tasks that are morally correct. This encyclopedia also states "*adokiraos*, even in these cases, always retains the meaning of rejection because of failure in trial.'" The Encyclopedia Britannica Dictionary defines the word as "to refuse to accept; reject (transitive verb) rejected as worthless or not standing a test: condemned."

So I take the phrase "unto every good work reprobate" to mean that we do not acknowledge the good works as genuine. Therefore, we are not genuine and are rejected because of our failure in the trails that come our way. When we convince ourselves that confession without works is enough and the lump sum of what we need to do as Christians, God says we are abominable and not genuine. We must complete our journey.

When babies take their first step, we know that it is the first of millions more to come. We all know and can remember that a child's first step is the most exhilarating and exciting, both to the parent and the child. The natural instinct of the child is to keep his eyes focused on the parent. The child walks to the parent, who is holding out her arms and cheering on the wavering babe. The problem comes when the child looks down at its feet or back to where he has been. He begins to trip and stumble and then comes the fall. The child will then look up to the parent as he is helped back onto his feet. Both the child and the parent know that this is the beginning of a long journey ahead. As the baby now begins to become a child and toddler, his life will be forever changed. Most children learn to walk at around one year old. The Wikipedia Online Encyclopedia states that the average life expectancy for people in the United States is 78.2 years. Some even push one hundred and beyond. In comparison, that first step is a very small fraction of what is to come. In the end none of us can remember our first step. We have become consumed with what is ahead and comes next in our life.

This is a reflection of how your spiritual walk should be. When you take your first step, you are thrilled and rejoicing along with your heavenly Father and all the angels in heaven. The next part is to focus constantly. You are to never stop looking forward to what is coming next, forgetting about the past and keeping your eyes locked on God the Father. When you begin to look down at yourself, where your feet are going or where you have already been, you begin to trip, stumble, and fall. The wonderful thing is that our heavenly Father is there to help you up if you allow him. So when you get up, remember, continue forward, keep your eyes locked on the Lord and where he is bringing you next. Don't look down or back. You have just taken your first step with many more to come and begun a journey of life, love, truth, true freedom, and fulfillment. Life as you know it will never be, or shouldn't ever be, the same again.

The sinner's prayer is awesome in helping people to take the first step in serving God. It is essential, however, that we remember and communicate clearly to the people we are ministering to (our brothers and sisters and God's children) that the prayer is the first step in a long, wonderful, meaningful, and fulfilling journey. Our journey takes us down to a narrow gate, and we need to be forever checking ourselves that we have not veered from that path. If we are not careful, we can veer over to the broad way that leads to destruction (Matthew 7:13–14). If we allow this to happen and never return to the narrow path, our first step does not do us much good. Our journey is ordained and planned by God and should be led by the one who is all knowing, all powerful, the creator of the journey and everything in it. Most importantly, God is the creator and redeemer of the one taking the journey. Our first step is essential in our walk with the Lord, but it is not the entire walk.

> We thank you, Lord, for your Word. You are inspiring and awesome in all that you do. Lord, help me to continue to grow in you. Help me to walk out the changes in my life that need to be made. Father, please forgive me for the times I have become offended with others when rebuking me or correcting me in love. I choose to forgive them and myself. Please, Lord, help me to keep my eyes focused on you. Lord God, I choose not to look back at where I have been. I choose not to dwell on the past but instead to look ahead at what you have next for me. God, I choose not to continue walking in my old ways that are worldly and do not line up with your Word. I commit to studying your Word, to continually learn more of who you are and what you desire of me. I pray that you would give me your divine revelation and understanding of your word. Thank you, Lord; you are always with me, helping me to walk forward on this journey that you have predestined. I love you, God, and give you all the glory. You alone, God, are truly worthy of all my praise.

You may want to write down notes on the chapter and thoughts responding to the prayer, such as listing changes in your life that you see need to be made, or confess areas of offence or write your own praise to the Lord. When you take the time to write it down, it helps you to start the process of change. Confession and recognition are vital steps of getting rid of unwanted things such as negative feelings or actions.

_____

_____

_____

_____

Faith in Action Questions

1. What scripture stands out most to me in this chapter?

_____

2. How can I apply this scripture to my life?

_____

_____

_____

3. "They profess that they know God; but in works they deny him, being abominable, and disobedient, and unto every good work reprobate" (Titus 1:16). How am I denying God in what I do?

_____

_____

4. What can I do to change that behavior?

_____

_____

5. "This witness is true. Wherefore rebuke them sharply, that they may be sound in the faith; Not giving heed to Jewish fables, and commandments of men, that turn from the truth" (Titus 1:13–14). Have I become offended or angry at someone for rebuking or trying to help me correct something in my life in love?

_____

6. Who?

_____

It is important to be willing to receive correction. None of us is perfect. It is our job as believers to help each other grow.

7. This is my prayer or confession of forgiveness of that person. This will bring release, growth, and healing to me:

_____

_____

_____

_____

8. Who can I help disciple and grow in his or her walk with the Lord?

_____

9. What can I do to help him or her learn to walk out his or her faith?

_____

_____

HONOR HIS WORD

As Christians we believe in the Lord. When we believe in him, we do as he taught and commanded us to do. Jesus blazed a trail of righteousness and purity. He showed us how to face our enemy and the problems that come up in life. He also showed us how to walk out our faith and treat all those around us, both friend and enemy. Jesus addressed every aspect of life. He taught about money, rulers, authorities, marriage, friends, enemies, Satan, and sin.

We need to begin looking at our lives and comparing them to the way Jesus taught that we ought to live. The Old Testament has much to say about the way we should live as well. Jesus himself said that he did not come to destroy the law but fulfill it (Mathew 5:17). When our way of doing things or our attitudes do not line up with the Word of God, we should be doing everything we can to change. We can cry out to the Lord to help us where we are unable. With the help of the Lord, we can begin to leave and remove the old self and begin working on picking up what God would have us to do. When we believe in Jesus, we believe what he taught and his way of life. We need to take a stand. Either we believe the Word of God or we do not. It is impossible to say that you believe in Jesus as the Son of God and the Bible to be the inspired Word of God and yet pick it apart. I see so many that will say they agree with one part of the Bible and not another. I am at wits' end to understand how someone can admit that he or she believes God is all powerful, all knowing, and the same yesterday, today, and forever yet say that the Word of God could be flawed or wrong in some way. So many times I have heard professing Christians say that they believe one part of the Bible, or most parts, but not all of it. These Christians will begin to list the parts that they do no agree with or the parts that they say are not for today. How could God be the same yesterday, today, and forever, yet say something that was not for now? Is he unchanging or not? Of course he is! Does he know all or not? Of course he does! So we believe he knows all and yet think some of his Word is wrong! If God knows all (and he does), then he does not make mistakes. God does not and cannot make mistakes; therefore no part of his Word is wrong! We try to justify our actions or desires by saying that certain parts of the Bible we do not want to line up with are not for today or we simply don't believe them. Just because you say you don't believe something is true or for today, it does not mean that it is not.

Let me illustrate this to you in a story. My family and I were living in New Hampshire. My brother met a wonderful woman and was about to be married in Idaho. So my husband and I decided to take our family vacation in Montana after attending my brother's wedding in Idaho. We rented a car, and after attending their wedding, we went to Yellowstone National Park. After we spent a few days there, we decided to visit some of our dear friends who were living in Livingston, Montana, at the time. After a wonderful visit with them, we were headed back to Idaho to catch our plane back home. The whole trip had gone perfectly smoothly. My husband, as usual, had informed me of all the speed limits and read the highway signs along the way. The next thing I knew, I was being pulled over. I could not imagine what for because as far as I knew, I was going the speed limit. The last thing I heard from Donnie was the speed limit was seventy-five. I was abiding by that. The car that pulled me over was an unmarked car with a small siren on top. Then out stepped a police officer. When he came to the window, he asked for my license and registration. I handed it over, and then he asked that all-too-familiar question: "Do you know why I pulled you over?" Honestly, I replied, "No, sir." He began to tell me I had been going seventy-five. "Well, yeah!" I blurted. After giving me a frustrated yet puzzled look, he then informed me that the speed limit was fifty-five. A big ball began to form in my throat as he told me the fine for it. He then informed me that I would have to pay the fine immediately, and if I disputed it, I would be held for two days until the next circuit judge came around. He took my license and registration and went back to his car. "I don't believe this!" I shouted to my husband. "This can't be happening; I think this guy is a con artist." In New Hampshire or any other state I had been, you get a ticket and pay the fine by mail or when you go to court. I had never heard of such a thing and so it couldn't be true. I began to tell Donnie that I didn't believe this man was a police officer or that any law would make you pay a fine immediately. "Maybe this is some guy playing a prank with a siren on top of his car." After thinking about my last brilliant deduction, I came to the conclusion a prankster probably would not have a uniform. Of course, I still refused to believe that there was a law that would make me pay a fine immediately. So he must be trying to get some extra cash on the side by scamming an out-of-state visitor. My husband told me he had some money stashed away and that he thought it was legitimate and that we better pay it or we would not make it back in time to catch our flight. I became furious. But I did as my husband said. As soon as the man left I, got out of the car and began to throw a childish fit. I believed I had just been swindled, and as far as I thought, I had not broken the law. When I finished my fit, we resumed our journey back. About twenty minutes later, we passed a speed limit sign that read 55 MPH, so we assumed that we actually had been speeding and we probably had passed a sign we both missed. When we got back to Idaho, we called our friends in Montana to tell them our mishap. Our friends confirmed the Montana law. Later I saw my driving report that confirmed my ticket.

As the process of me getting a ticket was unfolding, I was in total disbelief of the whole thing. First of all, I did not believe I was speeding. Secondly, I was unsure whether the man was an officer. For all I knew, he was trying to get a little money for himself on the side. Just because I chose not to believe that I was wrong and chose not to believe the laws were as they were in Montana did not make it so. My disbelief did not change the truth or the reality of the situation. If I had chosen to act on my disbelief and be stubborn instead of listening to the wise council of my husband, I would have wound up in a lot of trouble. I would have been arrested, put in front of a judge, missed my flight, hurt my family, and would have still had to pay the fine. Just because I did not know about the law or understand it, it did not mean the law didn't exist. My ignorance and disbelief in the law would not have made any difference to the judge. I would have had to pay for the consequences of my actions. It would have been his duty to uphold the law regardless of my opinion and belief. Your lack of belief does not change the truth; it only changes what the consequences of your actions will be. We all will pay for what we do whether it is good or bad (2 Corinthians 5:10). That is why it is so important to know and study God's Word.

God is our judge, and he is fair and just. If we choose not to believe his Word and walk how he has instructed us because we didn't believe it was true, or it does not line up with what we want, that does not mean we are not going to be held accountable. Just as my actions would have affected all those around me, your actions and choices affect those around you. For better or worse, you are making an impression. God's Word is like the Montana law; it does not change just because we don't like it, and it may seem inconvenient. God's Word is the truth—all of it—whether we want to see the truth or not. It is hard to see truth and admit it when it exposes our sin and the changes that need to be made in our lives. Even though it is hard to change, we must. Let's begin to look at what God says we need to be doing: "If any man serve me, let him follow me; and where I am, there shall also my servant be: if any man serve me, him will the Father honor" (John 12:26).

First of all, we need to decide to serve him. Think about the word *serve* and what true service is. The word *serve* is defined in the Encyclopedia Britannica Dictionary as " a: to be a servant to: attend b: to give the service and respect due to (a superior) c: to comply with the commands or demands of." When we serve God, we see that it means that we give him the respect due to him. What is due him? All of our respect! He made us, gave us our talents to survive, made everything around us, and sent his only begotten Son to die for our sins and then rose him up again so that we would have a living God to serve and not a dead idol. Now that we are fully aware of the respect due to him, it makes it so much easier to meet the next part of service. Let's see what the next part of the definition tells us: we need "to comply with his commands or demands." The Encyclopedia Britannica Dictionary states that comply means "to conform or adapt one's actions to another's wishes, to a rule, or to necessity." When we pledge to serve God, we are pledging to give God the respect he deserves and to conform or adapt our actions to God's commands and wishes.

How do we know what his commands or wishes are? First of all, read his book. He wrote us the perfect instruction manual that addresses every issue that will come up in life. Just in case that is not enough, he gave us a direct line to his throne room! It's called prayer. When we spend time each day in prayer—which we need to be doing—we are able to pour our heart out to him. In prayer we can honor God, give our petitions, and be still, waiting to hear his response, will, and wishes for our life. Waiting for God to respond is an essential part of prayer that many of us forget about, yet it is extremely important!

> Master, which is the great commandment in the law? Jesus said unto him, Thou shalt love the Lord thy God with all thy heart, and with all thy soul, and with all thy mind. This is the first and great commandment.
>
> Matthew 22:36

Jesus tells us that it is our duty to love God with everything inside of us. We need to put him first. When we do that, His will comes before ours. We begin to continuously seek Him and what He wants for us and act on that before anything else. Jesus was telling us that when we do this, we will meet the requirements of all the other commandments because we will be doing God's will, and His will won't lead us into sin but rather away from it. "If ye love me, keep my commandments" (John 14:15).

The Lord shows us again that true love is obedience to his Word. When we truly love the Lord, we will follow and serve him. We show God that we love him through our actions. Jesus truly confirmed the old adage "actions speak louder than words." Actions prove your heart.

> Then said Jesus unto his disciples, If any man will come after me, let him deny himself, and take up his cross, and follow me. For whosoever will save his life shall lose it: and whosoever will lose his life for my sake shall find it. For what is a man profited, if he shall gain the whole world, and lose his own soul? Or what shall a man give in exchange for his soul?
>
> Matthew 16:24–26

In Matthew 16:24 the Lord tells his disciples when we go after Jesus, we are to deny ourselves. Denying ourselves means to let go of our plans, desires, and will for our lives. Then he says take up his cross. What is his cross? The Father's will and plan. His cross is the predestined will and plan of Father God. Jesus's cross represents the washing away of sin and the old way of life and the beginning of the fulfillment of forgiveness and the new plans. When Jesus died on the cross, it was a completion of the payment for sin, the required sacrifice.

Jesus asks a very key question in this verse. "For what is a man profited, if he shall gain the whole world, and lose his own soul? Or what shall a man give in exchange for his soul?"

The point that he is trying to get across in this passage is anything that you can acquire in this world does not profit you if you are not serving and honoring God. Strong's interprets the word profit as "to be useful, i.e. to benefit." Everything you have is worthless. It has no real value. The world might say it does, but in reality—God's kingdom—it is absolutely worthless unless it is being used to do his will.

Most everything we do in our lives is out of habit, whether bad or good. Changing the things in our life that are not pleasing to God can be difficult and take time. God can deliver you instantly, although He does not always choose to. The Lord allows us to use the free will He has blessed us with to determine to do what is right. We learn a lot through our struggles. I know that I have personally learned a lot after going through struggles. What I learned in these times has stuck with me more than things I have learned in the easier times. These lessons help to launch us forward into the rest of our life. Breaking a habit is a decision that we have to make over and over again. Then we have to choose to do what is right over and over again continually until that behavior becomes a new habit.

It is our duty as Christians to follow after Jesus and to obey the Word of God. We are obligated to read His Word and pray. We are to follow that still, small voice that leads us. We are to give the Most High all the honor He deserves. We are to love everyone we see, meet, and know. It is essential that we lay our plans down and follow the plan God has for our life. When we choose to let go of our plans and desires, very quickly our heart longs and desires God's will. His will becomes our drive and happiness. The thing that most people don't understand is that when we are chasing our own dreams, looking for happiness, even when it comes, we want something else and are never truly happy. It is only when we let it go that we begin to feel true joy and happiness. True joy and fulfillment can only be found in the will of God. We can't ever see that as long as we are holding onto our dream. Yet as soon as we step out in faith and let it go, it becomes crystal clear. With every step you take in God's direction, the more peace and joy begin to flood your life.

> Father God, I thank you for you word and guidance. You are gentle and kind. God, I thank you for your mercy. Please help me to focus on your Word. Thank you, Lord, that as I draw closer to you, you will draw closer to me. Lord, I recognize that I have nothing and that life is not worth living if I don't have you. All that I am is in you. Lord, I choose to obey your Word and voice. I choose not to be swayed by those around me. I thank you for your peace and joy. Lord, I praise you for who you are. You are all powerful and all knowing. God, thank you for your plan for my life. I love you, Father, and I see the wonder and glory of your Word manifested all around me.

You can use the space provided below to write down notes or thoughts about the chapter.

_____

_____

_____

_____

FAITH IN ACTION QUESTIONS

> Master, which is the great commandment in the law? Jesus said unto him, Thou shalt love the Lord thy God with all thy heart, and with all thy soul, and with all thy mind. This is the first and great commandment.
>
> Matthew 22:36–38

1. Do I love God with all my heart, soul, and mind?

_____

2. How do I show it?

_____

_____

3. What area in my life am I not giving all to God?

_____

_____

4. What can I do to fix that?

_____

_____

_____

5. In what areas of my life am I not bringing honor to God and not showing Him that I love Him by breaking His commands?

_____

_____

6. What is the first step I can take in breaking my bad habit?

_____

_____

7. My prayer to God to help me lay down my old ways and take up his ways:

_____

_____

_____

_____

HONOR OTHERS

The greatest commandment of God is to love him with all your heart, soul, and mind. Jesus then goes on to state that the second greatest thing you can do is to love your neighbor as yourself. When God says something is important and a great commandment, we better listen. I think it is important that we figure out exactly what he means by it and how the best way to go about doing it is. We know that it is important to God, so it needs to become important to us. If it has not been a priority in the past, it is time to make it one. When our priorities line up with God's, everything seems to run smoother and fall into place. Time and time again, I tried to do things, fix things, or deal with people the way I saw fit. I never got anywhere until I gave it to God and did it his way.

"This is the first and great commandment. And the second is like unto it, Thou shalt love thy neighbor as thyself" (Mathew 22:38–39). The first thing we need to decide is who is our neighbor? Everyone is our neighbor—the people who live next to us, the people we work with, the people who work in the business next to us, the telemarketer, the person in line next to us, the people driving all around us, our neighboring counties, states, countries and the people living in them. Not only does it honor God and is part of our service to do this, but if you think about it, he made all of them. It helps to think about it in the light that every single person you meet is a child of God. He made them and loves them. When I think about it that way, it makes it easier to be nice to and love those around me. I mean, who in his or her right mind would want to mess with the family of the Most High, the Lord of all creation, and the most powerful in the universe? God even makes it clear to us: "Vengeance is mine" (Romans 12:19). I don't know about you, but I definitely don't want God taking out vengeance on me because I hurt one of his children. It is important to remember we should not allow fear to be our driving motivation. The love of God should be our motivation.

He loves and forgives everyone else just as much as you. People might do things that are different from you, but their sin is a sin just like your sin is a sin. No sin is better than any other; all are worthy of death! Praise God that he has washed it *all* away, ours and theirs. All we need to do is accept him as savior and master, obey Him, ask him for forgiveness, and forgive those around us so that we can receive his forgiveness.

God did not say that we have to agree with all people or even like everything they do. He made us all different so that we can accomplish the purpose set out for each of us. We can hate sin and love the person. Remember, God said, "Be angry and sin not" (Ephesians 4:26). Keep in mind that we are not perfect and God still loves us. We can disagree with people yet respect them and give them the love and honor they are due. They don't deserve it, you say! Well, neither do you or I. We are not doing it for them and others don't do it for us; we all do it for God. If we can get our minds wrapped around the fact that what we do for others we are doing for God, it would make doing his will a hundred times easier. This frame of mind can make it easy, fun, and exciting to love those around us.

How do we love others? We love them by treating them how God would. God meets our needs spiritually. So we need to be ministering to and disciplining others. It is important to help new believers grow. We can help them by recommending good scriptures. We can find out which ones would be the most helpful and relevant by asking them what is going on in their lives. All of us were excited when we first accepted the Lord, but we also had a lot of issues to work through. We will always have issues that we need to work on because no matter how had we try, we will never be perfect. The point is to strive to be the best we can and always quick to repent. If you have never read the Bible, it can be overwhelming and difficult to know where to begin. Even nonbelievers need ministry. We can show the love of God to anyone through the ministry of help and hospitality. No matter where you go, there is someone in need of a friend. People are hungry for relationships. Some people might need someone to vent to. Others may need advice or companionship. Many are starving to hear the Word of God.

God meets our physical needs. So as we see people in need we can help to meet their needs. You don't have to be rich to do this. Buy them some food if you can afford it or even if you can't. That is what faith is about. Many times God has asked me to do things I couldn't afford and I didn't know how I would pay for things. As I began to step out and commit to do it whether it looked as if I could or not, that's when God would step in and supernaturally provide. He is extremely creative and moves on your faith. When you buy them food, try to think about what they might want. It is not always necessary to go out and buy it; give some of yours. If you don't know anyone to help in this way, you can always donate to your local food pantry. Take some of the food from your pantry that has been there not getting eaten. Just be sure that it is not expired (junk is not a blessing). You can also meet their needs by buying them clothes. If you know someone unable to buy themselves clothes, take them on a shopping date either at a department store or a used clothing store. Remember, it is important to do your best. If you are able to give more, do it. Don't let the lack of money discourage you from helping. All of us have clothes in our closets that we have not worn for a long time. The reality is that we probably won't wear them again. So why not help yourself to unclutter while blessing others? Remember, junk is not a blessing. Don't be surprised if God even asks you to give your nicest or even some of your favorite outfits. Remember whatever you do for others, you are doing it for the Lord. If we think about this when we are doing something, or not doing something, for someone, we will do and give our best.

Tell the truth to everyone. Sometimes we excuse lies away as being necessary, helpful, or the right thing to do at the time. Lying is never helpful to anyone. When we lie, most of the time, it is because we are ashamed of something we have done. In some cases we just don't want to deal with others emotions if we don't agree. Sometimes we tell a lie trying to make someone feel better. This kind of helpfulness only lasts a little while. In the end the person will have realized the truth and ultimately be hurt worse in the end. Not only is it more painful later, but he or she has lost valuable time to change something. When we excuse our lies to be helpful to another, we are essentially lying to ourselves as well. The truth is we don't want to deal with looking bad. Or maybe we don't want to enter into a long, drawn-out conversation that could expose ourselves in a way that we don't want to. The devil wins on both sides in this situation. The person being lied to is unable to take necessary steps; you are sinning and allowing Satan to have a foothold in your life. This slows your own spiritual growth. The world tends to look at a white lie as something good and helpful—even necessary—on occasion. This is one of the biggest deceptions straight out of the pit of hell. I have read the Bible many times, and I have never read any classifications of a lie. There is no such thing as a good (white) lie. My Bible says: "Now the Spirit speaketh expressly, that in the latter times some shall depart from the faith, giving heed to seducing spirits, and doctrines of devils; Speaking lies in hypocrisy; having their conscience seared with a hot iron" (1 Timothy 4:1–2).

This scripture tells us that when we lie we are departing from our faith and paying attention to seducing spirits and doctrines of devils. When we speak a lie, it is in hypocrisy. The Greek word for hypocrisy is *hupokrisis* and is defined in the Strong's Greek Dictionary as "acting under a feigned part." When we allow this to happen, we allow our conscience to be "seared with a hot iron." The phrase "seared with a hot iron" in this verse is actually one word in the Greek. That word is *kausteriazo*, meaning "to brand" ("cauterize"), i.e., (by implication) to render unsensitive (figuratively). When something is cauterized, it stops the flow. Then that spot becomes unsensitive. So lying can essentially have our conscience no longer sensitive. When our conscience has no sensitivity, we are no longer sensitive to the flow or leading of the Holy Spirit.

> Lie not one to another, seeing that ye have put off the old man with his deeds; And have put on the new man, which is renewed in knowledge after the image of him that created him.
>
> Colossians 3:9–10

> Whiles it remained, was it not thine own? and after it was sold, was it not in thine own power? why hast thou conceived this thing in thine heart? Thou hast not lied unto men, but unto God.
>
> Acts 5:4

> A false witness shall not be unpunished, and he that speaketh lies shall not escape.
>
> Proverbs 19:5

When we lie, it is not only to men but God! We will all pay for our lies. God makes it clear that we can't escape from it. God's will is not for bad things to happen, but he did give us free will. If we choose to go against what is right and in his will, we will have to answer for it and deal with the punishment. God is fair and just. If he says that there is a consequence for a certain action, he must stick to them or he would be a liar himself. God is not a liar and can't lie. If he did not stick to his Word, he would not be just. God is just. Throughout the Bible God speaks of consequences or curses that will come on you if you are not obedient to his Word. Many people blame God for the things that happen to them when the truth is that they themselves are to blame. God did not make you do the thing; you chose to do it. When you get a speeding ticket, is it the officer's fault? No, he did not speed; you did. When your child gets grounded, is it your fault? No, it is your child's. She chose the action, and you were obligated to enforce the punishment for bad behavior. The punishment is not meant to bring harm but rather good to the child. It exposes the wrong choice and prayerfully will help her to make the right choice in the future. We will talk about this a little more in chapter eight.

"In hope of eternal life, which God, that cannot lie, promised before the world began" (Titus 1:2, KJV). God is truth; he can't tell a lie and neither should we. We are to follow in his example. God picks us up when we are down. So we can encourage others and speak health and love into each others' life. We can stop putting the things that others say and do down. The Lord commands us to build each other up.

The Lord has strategically placed all of us. He has placed us where He wants us so that we can learn, grow, and be a help to those around us. One way the Lord has commanded us to help is by exhorting others. He tells us this in Hebrews 3:13: "But exhort one another daily, while it is called Today; lest any of you be hardened through the deceitfulness of sin." First of all, the scripture tells us to do this daily. *Daily* is an important part that we need to remember and be making a conscience effort to do. If the Lord tells us to do it daily, that means He has placed an opportunity for us to do so. We need to begin looking for and recognizing these opportunities when they arise. God did not tell us to do it when we felt like it. He states this not only for the benefit of others but for our benefit as well. When we take our focus off ourselves and place it on others in a positive way, we feel better as well. When we exhort others, we are to encourage them. We build them up and help them to do what is right. Many of us have this concept backward. We think that it is exhorting someone when we are comforting him to wallow in self-pity or helping him to justify his sinful actions. That is not exhortation. It is feeding the fear of rejection in yourself and allowing sin to continue. You are not exhorting or helping him in any way; you are actually doing more damage. I am not saying that we need to start slamming people when they are down or off track. I am saying in love we can encourage them in the right direction. Allow God to give us the words to speak. When people are on track or taking a step in the right direction, we can exhort them to keep going. We can help them by giving them the tools they need. Sometimes it is most helpful to others when we give them a testimony of when we were in the same or similar situation. It can encourage them that they are not alone. Tell them how God helped you through the situation and the steps that you took in the right direction that helped. Or share what you did wrong so that they don't make the same mistake. Allow God to use everything for good. The Bible says Jesus was made human. I believe this is so he is able to aid us when we are tempted because He was also tempted. Jesus can help because He has walked through the same things and found to be perfect. We have His example to follow.

And whosoever shall compel thee to go a mile, go with him twain. Give to him that asketh thee, and from him that would borrow of thee turn not thou away. Ye have heard that it hath been said, Thou shalt love thy neighbor, and hate thine enemy. But I say unto you, Love your enemies, bless them that curse you, do good to them that hate you, and pray for them which despitefully use you, and persecute you.

Matthew 5:41–44

We as Christians have to remember we are not supposed to be doing things the way everyone else in the world does it. Who cares what others think and say? God is the one we answer to and will face in the end. Not only are we supposed to help and show God's love to those who hate you, mistreat you, make fun of you, and torment you for your beliefs, we are supposed to do more for people than they even ask for. Why would anyone notice anything different about you (your relationship with the Almighty) if you only do the bare minimum? Most people slide by the skin of their teeth. The world says, "Do only the requirement." God says, "Do more." When we do what God commands, people will stop and meditate on why we did that. When we do only what was required, they won't give it another thought.

When we help others, we are honoring God. Therefore, it should be something we desire to do. Loving others and giving them the honor they deserve is good in so many ways. When we do things for others, it is meeting a commandment of God. It also makes a huge difference in the life of that person. He or she is affected spiritually, physically, and emotionally. That person is drawn to the love of God in you and will desire that same relationship with the Father. God is pleased because it is also done for Him. Not only does it help the other person and please God, it helps you as well. When you are concentrating on others' needs, you turn your focus off yourself. When this happens, you receive peace. You are no longer thinking about the struggles and attacks that are going on in your life. It stops you from being drawn in by fear, worry, and becoming jealous of others.

> Praise you, God, for your mercy and love. Lord, help me to see others as you see them. Thank you, Lord. You are perfect, and you love me despite my imperfections. Lord, forgive me for being judgmental of others. God, I repent for not truly loving your children. I repent for my treatment and gossip of others. Please help me to live my life to bring honor to you by giving honor and respect to those around me. Lord, I ask that you would continue to show me the things that you would have me to do. I commit to seeking your will and looking for the doors you open for me and opportunities you give me to be your hands and feet. Thank you, Lord, that you give me the opportunity to show others who you are and to serve you by serving others. You are so awesome, God. You are truly worthy of honor. Lord, your mercy endures forever. Thank you, Lord. You are so creative and have made each one of us different. Praise you, Master, that you have a plan and a purpose for me. Father, I thank you for making me special. I believe that with you, Lord, all things are possible, so with your help I can love others where they are at.

You can use the space provided below to write down notes or thoughts about the chapter or prayer.

_____

_____

_____

_____

Faith in Action Questions

1. What kinds of behaviors in people irritate me?

_____

_____

Lord, help me to have love for others despite these behaviors. I lift these irritations up to you and ask that you would give me peace and love in my heart. Help me minister your love and truth.

2. Who around me have I not treated as a child created by God and worthy of honor?

_____

3. What can I do next time I see him/her to show him/her God's love?

_____

_____

4. Who is in my life that I can help exhort, encourage, and lift up? What can I say to them?

_____

_____

5. What areas in my life have I not done wholeheartedly and to the best of my ability when asked to do it?

_____

6. What could I do to improve or go the extra mile in these areas?

_____

_____

7. How can I be a better example of the love of God?

_____

_____

HONOR THE LORD WITH YOUR TIME

God has a plan for your life. He has everything mapped out. His will for your life is perfect. God Almighty has planned a time for everything. If we truly want to experience total peace, joy, and the fulfillment of our purpose and ministry, we can stop planning our lives and begin letting the maker of time and all things guide us in his plan and in his timing. Even when we are in the middle of a crisis or something that seems like we just can't make it through, God has a plan for it. When we can't see the outcome and the timing seems the worst, we have full assurance that the timing is perfect and this is a time for us to grow and shine. Every circumstance, good or bad, in our lives has a purpose. Praise God!

Each and every one of us has a choice of the outcome in every situation that we face. We can either choose to walk through it God's way, or we can choose the path of destruction. When we choose to handle a situation the way God has instructed us we should, we are enabling the Holy Spirit to move. When we choose the path of destruction (not God's way), we are wasting valuable time. When we do things we know are not right because we think it will get us out of an uncomfortable situation quicker, we actually spend more time fixing the mess it creates.

Our Creator made seasons not only in weather but also in our lives. During these seasons we experience different things that help us to grow and launch us into the next phase. Just as in nature, God has orchestrated everything perfectly to flow from one thing to the next. We are all intertwined in a web that makes life possible. Every detail is orchestrated beautifully. When we begin to take ourselves out of the middle of things and look at it from an outside perspective, we can begin to see the bigger picture and can better appreciate our circumstances. It all comes back to taking the focus off ourselves and putting it on others and the Almighty's plan.

> To every thing there is a season, and a time to every purpose under the heaven: A time to be born, and a time to die; a time to plant, and a time to pluck up that which is planted; A time to kill, and a time to heal; a time to break down, and a time to build up; A time to weep, and a time to laugh; a time to mourn, and a time to dance; A time to cast away stones, and a time to gather stones together; a time to embrace, and a time to refrain from embracing; A time to get, and a time to lose; a time to keep, and a time to cast away A time to rend, and a time to sew; a time to keep silence, and a time to speak; A time to love, and a time to hate; a time of war, and a time of peace
> Ecclesiastes 3:1–8

Take time to honor God before you do anything else with your time. No time can be more valuable than spending it to honor God. Or by seeking his will and asking him, "What time is it?" How should I be spending my time? What season or timing is this in my life? God will show you if you take the time to listen and watch for his response. It is definitely worth seeking his will. When we don't, we seem to wander aimlessly around in circles and wonder if and when we are going to get out. Everything we try and do renders no fruit. In the end we are wasting precious time. Seeking God is our personal shortcut. If you want out of a situation or need to see results that are satisfying, do it right the first time. Time spent seeking God is never wasted. You will always get the best way through any situation.

Every thing that we do for the Lord is honoring to Him. Things done for Him can be done outwardly and inwardly. Both are a sacrifice of our time to bring Him honor. In Ephesians 6:12, it clearly states that we are not fighting against flesh and blood (physical things) but against spiritual things such as principalities, powers, and spiritual wickedness. When we war against these things, it is done in our hearts and minds. We are fighting a battle of spiritual warfare. We are constantly making a choice between doing what the Lord wills, what He has commanded, and what we know in our hearts to be right, or choosing to do what Satan would have us to do and making the same choices the rest of the world does. This entire battle goes on in our minds and is not seen in the physical. Only the outcome of the battle is seen. We fight this battle every day for the glory of our Lord. Every little thing we do is important. Little things in life are what lead up to and are the stepping stones for the great things. Every outcome is seen by all those around us and tells a story. So fight the good fight and know that we can all win because we have

God on the inside, and He is greater than anything that can come against us.

Hosea 10:12 tells us, "Sow to yourselves in righteousness, reap in mercy; break up your fallow ground: for it is time to seek the LORD, till he come and rain righteousness upon you." We honor the Lord by asking him what to do in every area of our lives. There is no greater sacrifice we can give Him than our life and will. When we ask God the Father what we should be doing or what he wants us to be doing, we are telling him, "I know you are wiser and more powerful than anyone or anything, and I value your opinion and will for my life over any other, including mine." When you seek the Lord, you are praising him for who he is. When we do this, God will "rain righteousness upon you." You will be covered in righteousness, or be made right and moral.

Until we are seeking the Lord in what we do, we are walking blind. It is as if we are walking around blindfolded trying to find the target. We can compare it to pin the tail on the donkey. When we get blindfolded and spun around, we have no idea where the donkey's tail is because we have lost sense of direction and can't see what is in front of us. Everyone is laughing as we place our tail on a spot we have picked. And when the blindfold is taken off, we can see that we were either way off or just a little. Either way, it is not where it belongs, and close enough is not good enough. A donkey has no use for a tail unless it is where God created it. Those around us will give us a prize if we were closer than anyone else, but it is still no use to the donkey.

Without the guidance of Jesus, we are walking blindfolded. God is waiting for us to get it right. He looks on, waiting patiently, and those around us laugh at our struggle. When we put things in place where we think they should be, they do not always hit the mark. Unless things are done properly, in order and in God's timing, they don't work properly. Or they can't function at all and our effort was useless. The world may say you have done well enough and even award you with something that has no eternal value. But if we seek the Lord and take the blindfold off, we can see clearly and accomplish our mission in a timely fashion and hit the mark. Then we will store up treasure in heaven that will last for all eternity.

Seeking the Lord is extremely important, so seek the Lord in where He wants you to plant. The soil where the seeds are planted needs to be fertile and free of rocks and weeds. Before seeds are planted, there has to be some preparation done. This takes time. The Lord knows the hearts (soil) of all. If you seek the Lord where to plant and sow, you will reap a harvest that you can't contain. God knows where the best ground for you is. When you sow without seeking God, you risk wasting your seed. It could produce nothing and get choked out. We are not all knowing, but God is. We can be wise and seek the one who knows all.

> And he spake many things unto them in parables, saying, Behold, a sower went forth to sow; And when he sowed, some seeds fell by the way side, and the fowls came and devoured them up: Some fell upon stony places, where they had not much earth: and forthwith they sprung up, because they had no deepness of earth: And when the sun was up, they were scorched; and because they had no root, they withered away. And some fell among thorns; and the thorns sprung up, and choked them: But other fell into good ground,

and brought forth fruit, some an hundredfold, some sixtyfold, some thirtyfold.

Matthew 13:3–8

When we seek God, we awaken our spirit. The Bible says we will arise from the dead. We will be able to walk with diligence and wisdom that can only come from on high. We will also get back lost time. We are commanded to walk wisely and do these things and reap the blessing of time redeemed in Ephesians 5:14–16: "Wherefore he saith, Awake thou that sleepest, and arise from the dead, and Christ shall give you light. See then that ye walk circumspectly, not as fools, but as wise, Redeeming the time, because the days are evil." In this verse, we are told to walk circumspectly. The Greek word for circumspectly is *akribos* and is translated in the Strong's Greek Dictionary as "exactly." When we do things exactly, we take the time needed to make sure it is done without flaw. So this verse is telling us that it is important to be wise in our walk and take the time to make sure we are doing exactly what we are supposed to be. Do not rush full bore ahead without thinking or consulting God first; this is how fools walk out their lives.

Whatever you care about, you will put your time and energy into. Someone who loves classic cars will spend all his extra time tinkering on it and restoring it. If you love money, you will work extra hard and have a hard time leaving work. Someone who loves the Lord will spend his or her free time seeking him, worshiping him, studying his Word, and doing his will.

Love worketh no ill to his neighbour: therefore love is the fulfilling of the law. And that, knowing the time, that now it is high time to awake out of sleep: for now is our salvation nearer than when we believed. The night is far spent, the day is at hand: let us therefore cast off the works of darkness, and let us put on the armour of light. Let us walk honestly, as in the day; not in rioting and drunkenness, not in chambering and wantonness, not in strife and envying. But put ye on the Lord Jesus Christ, and make not provision for the flesh, to fulfil the lusts thereof.

Romans 13:10–14

The book of Romans tells us that we should know that now is the time to stop sleeping. When we are sleeping, we are unaware of the things that are going on around us. When we are unaware and not really paying attention, our defenses get lowered. That is when we can really get slammed. Things tend to hit us a lot harder when we are thrown off guard. So wake up! Put on your armor and be alert. Use the protection God has given you; it does no good collecting dust. Good armor is dented armor. You can always tell a soldier who is in active duty compared to inactive. The soldier who is active has a wrinkled or dirty uniform that doesn't look the greatest. An inactive soldier might look better on the outside because his uniform has nice, crisp creases. His boots are shiny, and not one thing is out of place. I ask you, who would you rather have on your side? The soldier who is fully aware of the battle and the things necessary to fulfill his mission or the one who is unaware yet looks the part? Let's wake up and honor God with our time. Let's be aware of our mission and what we need to complete it. Let's be aware of all that is going on around us and every opportunity placed in front of us by the Lord.

Christians as a whole have fallen asleep. We are

completely unaware of the things that are going on around us. We have become so busy with our own life and worldly things that we don't realize what is going on in the lives of our children, our homes, our churches, schools, towns, our state, country, and around the world. Sin is prevalent, and we don't even recognize it anymore. Our freedoms are being stripped away, and we are too busy to get involved. If we don't begin to take action now, before we realize what is going on, we won't be able to preach the Word of God in church, and our children will be turning us in to the government for practicing our beliefs. You might think this is a little farfetched and we are not even close to this happening. I am telling you we are closer than you think. I bet the Jews were saying the same thing as more and more segregation laws were passed until one day they were no longer free themselves. Do not sit around and watch all this happen. Stand up, take action, and speak up for what you believe in.

> Praise you, God, for you are the Alpha and Omega. You have made time and given me time to figure out the truth. Lord, help me to use my life and the time you have given me wisely. Lord, I give you each and every day of the rest of my life. I want to spend my time honoring you. I choose to put you first and believe that you will work out the rest. Thank you, Lord, that when I take the time to spend with you that your grace is multiplied in my life. Father, I thank you for sending your Son to die for us. Thank you for taking time to make me and invest in me. Help me, Lord, to take the time to minister to others and put you first in my life. Thank you for the

seasons in my life. I give you all the honor and glory.

You can use the space provided below to write down notes or thoughts about the chapter or prayer.

_____

_____

_____

_____

FAITH IN ACTION QUESTIONS

1. What do I do in my free time?

_____

_____

2. How much time do I spend with God?

_____

3. What are some unnecessary activities I participate in?

_____

4. How much time do I spend on unimportant things?

_____

5. What can be eliminated out of my free time to make place for God?

_____

_____

6. What can be eliminated to make time for my family?

_____

7. What areas in my life have I fallen asleep (lazy or unaware) that need to be reawakened?

_____

_____

Honor the Lord with Money

We need to keep in mind that nothing we have came from anywhere but the Lord Almighty himself. We could gain nothing and do nothing if it were not for him. God made us, gave us our talents, and put opportunities before us. God is the only one who deserves glory in our lives. Sometimes it is easy to forget that he alone is our provider. It can be easy to puff ourselves up and say how hard we worked to earn a living, what a good job we have done, and that we deserve all that we have. The truth of the matter is we were all sinners and deserved nothing but death. It is through God's grace and pleasure in us that he blesses us. He does want to bless us! Not because we deserve it but because he loves us so much. Praise God.

We must come into the frame of mind that what we have is not truly ours but given to us by the Lord to be stewards of it. All that we have in our possession is God's, and we are the managers. When you can fully wrap your mind around this concept, life becomes so much more fulfilling and less stressful. If you own nothing, you have nothing to lose. It becomes easier to give things and money away. You will begin to wait and listen for the Lord before you spend or do anything. It becomes so awesome to sit back and watch God work through you. Miracles become more evident and so does his awesome love and grace. Numbers will not add up, and that is okay. God's ways are not ours (he does not do math the same way). God always pays his bills, not us. When money is needed, it always comes. As you allow God to run his finances through you, it becomes clear that you are becoming a faith giant.

"And he said unto them, Render therefore unto Caesar the things which be Caesar's, and unto God the things which be God's" (Luke 20:25, KJV). This statement made by Jesus makes it crystal clear that we need to pay taxes and give the church the tithe from the money that the Lord provides for us to use for his glory. I want to take this verse apart and explore it a bit further. The Greek word for *render* is *apodidomi*. This word means "to give away," for example, up, over, *back*, etc. If we substitute "give back" in place of *render*, we can clearly see the money was not ours in the first place. The government printed the money, therefore part needs to be given back, and the Lord provided it so we need to give his money back to him. It is only transferred to us for a short time so that we might use it to do His will so that He would receive honor and glory.

"But this I say, He which soweth sparingly shall reap also sparingly; and he which soweth bountifully shall reap also bountifully. Every man according as he purposeth in his heart, so let him give; not grudgingly, or of necessity: for God loveth a cheerful giver" (2 Corinthians 9:6–7). It is a principle laid out by the Lord from the foundations of the Earth. The more you put into something, the more you will get out of it. This principle can be applied to every aspect of life. The more seeds you plant, the more vegetables, herbs, and flowers will grow. The more things you give away, the more things come your way. The more money you give away, the more the Lord provides. The more spiritual knowledge you give away, the more divine revelation, understanding, faith, and authority you receive back. One key part of this scripture I think many of us forget is that we are not supposed to only give out of necessity (obligation), but we need to do it because it makes us happy to serve God.

Even if at first you begin to give out of sheer obedience, you will soon begin to realize that it makes you happy to give. This is a hard concept to really explain. You can't really understand the feeling you get until you begin to do it. You begin to feel better about yourself and life altogether.

> Will a man rob God? Yet ye have robbed me. But ye say, Wherein have we robbed thee? In tithes and offerings. Ye are cursed with a curse: for ye have robbed me, even this whole nation. Bring ye all the tithes into the storehouse, that there may be meat in mine house, and prove me now herewith, saith the LORD of hosts, if I will not open you the windows of heaven, and pour you out a blessing, that there shall not be room enough to receive it.
>
> Malachi 3:8–10

The way money controls people and their decision making has gotten out of control. Money has become an idol in many people's lives. God hates idols and hates us to serve them, and so do I. It turns my stomach how people can serve it. We will turn to money to decide if we can help this person. What will I gain? How will the outcome be financially? Will I lose? If I lose money, what will happen next? Because of lack of faith, we decide, *Well, sorry, God. I can't serve you today. I hope you understand it is not financially sound. You understand, right? I have my future, my children, family, and retirement to think about. If I do this, what else might I have to do? What else will it cost me? I think I better just stop now. Maybe tomorrow I can serve you, God, instead of giving money. Lord, I hope you don't mind when I sang on Sunday and said "I give you my all and all." I meant all but my money. Maybe next time you can ask me to do something that does not cost so much or is not so out of the way.* When reading this you might say, "That is ridiculous; I would never think or say anything like that to God." The truth is you don't have to say it. Your actions say it for you. The way you treat people and handle the situations and tests in your life tell God exactly how you think and feel. Not only are you telling God you are not willing to serve Him, but God says that you will walk in a curse if you rob him of what is his. So quit letting money lead you and start letting God.

Money is not bad; we all need it. God wants us to walk in financial blessing as well. We just have to be so careful not to let the love or need of money consume us. We can do things in our life that can help us financially. Some of those things include sticking to a budget and not letting our spending exceed our income. We definitely need to be good stewards of what God has given us to use and manage in our lives. Money is included in this. There are many different tools available to manage our finances. The thing we need to get a handle on is to have a balance between managing our money and not being consumed by it. We can't be consumed with money and be consumed with God at the same time.

Lord, thank you that I don't have to be concerned for my needs. You are amazing, God, how you work everything out. I pray that your children will wake up and see the selfish needs and desire for more money is an idol. It becomes what we serve if we are not careful to keep our heart in check. Lord, please help me to lay down my fear of not having financial stability and help me to truly see I have no future or rest (retirement) if it is not in you. Lord, help me to truly serve you in love for one another instead of the love of money. God Almighty, I lay down my desires and need for fleshly comfort and worldly success to truly feel real success in you alone. To my sovereign leader, give me the strength to hold my shield of faith high that the fiery darts of the evil one will not penetrate me. Lord, I give you thanks for guiding me and being my Jehovah Jireh (provider). I believe that you will give me all that I need and more to fulfill the purposes you have for me. I know that as I walk in obedience that I will be blessed in everything, including my finances. So I choose to focus on you and not money. Thank you, Lord, for helping me to take every thought captive that tells me, "You can't make it if you do as God has commanded." I cast it out as a vain imagination. Lord, I choose to line my thoughts up with your Word and step out in faith with my finances to see what an awesome God you truly are. Thank you, Lord, that if I allow it, you show me how powerful you are and remind me that you are in control of everything, including the money in my possession for a time. I choose to trust you and not live in fear and anxiety of losing my money or not having enough of it. I love you, Lord, and I repent for making money an idol in my life. I choose now and forevermore to lay it down and only serve you, the one true God. Praise you, Father.

You can use the space provided below to write down notes or thoughts about the chapter or prayer.

_____

_____

_____

_____

FAITH IN ACTION QUESTIONS

1. Is there any area in my life that I am holding back money from going where it belongs?

_____

2. How far am I in debt?

_____

3. At the rate I am going, how long will it be until I am out of debt?

_____

4. Am I sticking to a budget?

_____

5. What areas am I spending money that is not good for me?

_____

6. Am I making the love of money an idol in my life by putting it before people?

_____

7. In what way can I begin to change this?

_____

_____

_____

8. Am I holding anything back from the Lord because of fear?

_____

IMPORTANT SCRIPTURES

Many of us have our favorite scriptures that we read or quote over and over again to help build us up spiritually. There is nothing wrong with having a favorite scripture or a life scripture to help you. The problem comes when you oust the rest of it. We need to remember that there is an entire book. It is extremely important to feed your soul with God's Word daily. We all need fresh understanding and revelation so that we can grow continually. None of us could live on eating the same food for breakfast, lunch, and dinner for the rest of our lives. We can't live on the same spiritual food either. We need to be reading the whole Bible and listening for the voice of God.

We can't truly live unless we have the Word of God. When Jesus is being tempted by Satan in the wilderness, He makes a very powerful and important statement to Satan: "But he answered and said, It is written, Man shall not live by bread alone, but by every word that proceedeth out of the mouth of God" (Matthew 4:4). If we eat and drink, our bodies will continue to move. I ask you, are you defined by your flesh or what you look like? Or are you defined by what you do, say, the way you treat others, and what you believe? Our bodies are not who we are; therefore, we (our spirit) can't live by bread alone but by the Word of God.

Without God's Word, we are spiritually dead. This does not only pertain to eternal life but here on Earth as well. Think about it. How much did you truly enjoy life before you knew the Lord? Life was not enjoyed very much, if any, at all. We wandered around day to day plugging along. Some of us were doing the same thing day in and day out. Can you remember the feeling that life was empty and pointless? Some of us had so much hurt in the past that we tried drowning it away with alcohol, drugs, sex, and work. We were no longer enjoying life, only waiting till it was over. We tried filling our emptiness with stuff, things like money, toys, chocolate, entertainment, and people.

Something happened when we heard the truth and finally chose to accept Jesus as our Lord and Savior. That void that seemed to gnaw at the pit of our stomach for as long as we could remember began to disappear. The more we searched through God's Word and talked with other believers, the more purpose we began to feel in our life. God's Word began to come alive, and we began to see that He knew us intimately.

The closer we get to the Lord, the more we feel that empty space disappearing, and it should drive us to want more and more of Him. Deuteronomy 13:4 tells us what we should be doing once we receive the truth: "Ye shall walk after the Lord your God, and fear him, and keep his commandments, and obey his voice, and ye shall serve him, and cleave to him." Walking after the Lord leads us on the path to eternal life. Fearing the Lord is the beginning of knowledge. Keeping his commandments betters our life and proves our love and faith in him. Serving him leads to fullness, and cleaving to him is how we get to know him more. The Hebrew word for cleave is *dabaq* and is defined in Strong's Hebrew-Aramaic Dictionary as "to impinge, i.e., cling or adhere; figuratively, to catch by pursuit." So when we are catching the Lord by pursuit, he draws closer to us and we form an intimate relationship.

> Go to now, ye that say, Today or tomorrow we will go into such a city, and continue there a year, and buy and sell, and get gain: Whereas ye know not what shall be on the morrow. For what is your life? It is even a vapour, that appeareth for a little time, and then vanisheth away. For that ye ought to say, If the Lord will, we shall live, and do this, or that. But now ye rejoice in your boastings: all such rejoicing is evil. Therefore to him that knoweth to do good, and doeth it not, to him it is sin.
>
> James 4:13–17

We all have hopes, dreams, and desires for our lives. We set goals and strive to reach them. God wants us to make sure these plans line up with his will. God wants us to acknowledge the fact that he is omniscient. He knows what is best. He alone knows when we will die and what will happen tomorrow. When we rejoice in our own plan and in ourselves, it is evil. We need to be rejoicing in the Lord.

We all have opinions and think things need to be done our way. A lot of us think it is our obligation to tell others what they are doing wrong. We might not even tell them; instead we might criticize them internally or to others. The Bible warns against judging others in Matthew 7:1–2: "Judge not, that ye be not judged. For with what judgment ye judge, ye shall be judged: and with what measure ye mete, it shall be measured to you again." It is important to seek God and search our hearts to see if they are out of God's will or if it is just something that we don't like or would not do ourselves. We need to be careful when we are trying to correct or rebuke someone that we are truly doing it in love. When God shows us an area in someone's life that needs work, he is doing it so that we can help and pray for him, not so we can judge him. If he refuses to listen, then we have a tendency to tell all those around us how we feel on the matter and that we wished the other person would just do it right. Well, God made us all different, and each of us does things differently. We need to remember we have all made plenty of our own mistakes. It is okay to offer others advice, especially if they are seeking it. We all need to be careful not to cross the line and begin to judge them. It is a fine line and easy to cross it. So be sure just to give yourself a check.

Many times when we are walking out our everyday lives, we seem to forget that when we accepted Jesus as our Savior and chose to follow him and do his will, God through his Holy Spirit came to live in us. If we allow God, he is there with us giving us the strength and wisdom to do anything that he has called us to do. Jesus reminds us of this when he says in Matthew 19:26, "But Jesus beheld them, and said unto them, With men this is impossible; but with God all things are possible." Therefore, what may seem impossible with our natural eyes is completely possible because it is not us doing it but rather God in us. It can be easy to feel God on Sunday and remember that He is there, but the rest of the week we struggle. Remember, God does not forget about us the rest of the week. We are the ones who forget about Him. God is waiting there until you call on him and recognize him. We need to be making every day conscience efforts to spend time with God and recognize him and what he can and will do.

> For a good tree bringeth not forth corrupt fruit; neither doth a corrupt tree bring forth good fruit. For every tree is known by his own fruit. For of thorns men do not gather figs, nor of a bramble bush gather they grapes. A good man out of the good treasure of his heart bringeth forth that which is good; and an evil man out of the evil treasure of his heart bringeth forth that which is evil: for of the abundance of the heart his mouth speaketh. And why call ye me, Lord, Lord, and do not the things which I say?
>
> Luke 6:43–46

The Lord clearly shows us a way to discern what is in others' hearts as well as ours if we take the time to look. It is important that we regularly take a look at our heart and life. Meditate on the things you have said and done. Ask yourself, "Does this line up with the Word of God?" If not, think about where you went wrong and what you might have let creep into your heart. Repent of it and move on to do the things that are pure and righteous. You might have to put a bridle on your tongue and think about everything you say before you say it until it becomes a habit and way of life again to bring forth good fruit. We must take every thought captive and decide whether to accept or reject it. The Lord makes a very powerful statement in Luke 6:46: "And why call ye me, Lord, Lord, and do not the things which I say?" If we truly call him the Lord of our life, then we must submit to his Word. In Greek the word Lord is *kurios*. It comes from the Greek word *kuros* (supremacy); supreme in authority, i.e., (as noun) controller; by implication, Master (as a respectful title). So when we call him Lord, we are calling him master, controller, and the supreme authority in our life. The supreme authority is always the one who makes the decisions and tell his servants what is to be done. When we call Jesus Lord, we are acknowledging the fact that He is our supreme authority and we are His servants.

> And he said unto them, When ye pray, say, Our Father which art in heaven, Hallowed be thy name. Thy kingdom come. Thy will be done, as in heaven, so in earth. Give us day by day our daily bread. And forgive us our sins; for we also forgive every one that is indebted to us. And lead us not into temptation; but deliver us from evil.
>
> Luke 11:2–4

None of us seems to have any trouble remembering that Jesus forgives. We constantly remind each other that it is okay when we mess up because God's grace and forgiveness covers our sin. Then we tell each other, "Dust off your feet and move on." This is all true. The problem comes in where we forget that we are supposed to be forgiving others so that we will receive the forgiveness from the Lord. Forgiving others is necessary so that we can be forgiven. The one person that gets hurt the most from not forgiving is the person not willing to forgive.

Remember, God comes before anyone. We need to realize that without God we are nothing. We would not even exist. It is important to put everything of this world aside to focus on God if we are to be His disciples and follow Him. We need a complete change in life. Jesus tells us in Luke 14:26–27, "If any man come to me, and hate not his father, and mother, and wife, and children, and brethren, and sisters, yea, and his own life also, he cannot be my disciple. And whosoever doth not bear his cross, and come after me, cannot be my disciple." The word *hate* in this text is the Greek word *miseo*, and the Strong's Greek Dictionary defines it as "to detest (especially to persecute); by extension, to love less." We are to love everyone less than we love God. We are not on this earth to please all those around us. We are here to please God and do as God has commanded and planned for us. We are reminded of this in Galatians 1:10, "For do I now persuade men, or God? Or do I seek to please men? For if I yet pleased men, I should not be a servant of Christ." Paul is making a very important point in this scripture. Paul is pointing out that we are to think about pleasing God and not men. Our society has gotten us so wrapped around this idea of having to please everyone, including ourselves. We worry about what people think we look like, about what they will think if we do this or that. Who cares? Not one of them created us and not one of them can give us salvation! We have become so laid back that this worldly point of view has taken over our minds and activities in the church.

Christians worry what other members might think if we are truthful or what new believers might think or do if they are told the full gospel to start. What if they don't come back? Well, I ask, what will happen to them if they are not told? The truth is if you don't tell them to start, you never will, and if they happen to hear it later on, it might cause more problems; they might die before they are told. If someone wants to serve the Lord, who are we to decide when he is ready to start? That, I believe, is between him and the Lord. It is our job to give him the tools necessary. People are a lot stronger and smarter than we tend to give them credit for. If we are consumed with pleasing man, then we may never share the truth for fear of what they will think. The truth is most people will respect you for telling the truth and giving your opinion knowing that they might not agree. They will actually listen to you more carefully because they respect you. Most importantly, God will honor you.

We worry about what people might think when we are worshiping God and doing his work. Many Christians worry what people will think if they raise their hands to worship or if they don't raise their hands. Are we worshiping the congregation or God Almighty? Some denominations critique other churches because they are to wild for dancing and raising their hands. The denominations that say you should raise your hands critique others for not truly being free to worship because they don't raise their hands. I say everyone is wrong. We are to be worshiping God and to do that sometimes he leads us to raise our hands; sometimes he leads us to stand still in his presence; sometimes he leads us to shout with joy, sometimes sit and others stand. We are all one body, are we not? We worry what others will think if we participate in an activity or we don't participate. We simply can't do everything others expect us to. We must always be led by the spirit of God. That is not to say you should sit back und do nothing because you have not heard the voice of God say to do it specifically. If you listen and watch for the Lord, he will show the direction he wants you to go. Some activities fall in and others don't. It is time to quit bickering over the little stuff and making a doctrine out of everything. The important thing is that we are all striving to meet the same goal: to serve the Lord Jesus and to complete His will in our lives and on this Earth.

Those around us should be able to tell that God lives in us. They should see the way that we act and the things that we do are different and better. Remember from chapter one that Jesus himself told us to do this in Matthew 5:16: "Let your light so shine before men, that they may see your good works, and glorify your Father which is in heaven." This will draw them to seek out the Lord and give him glory for the things that they see him doing in our lives. What we do speaks so much more to people than what we say. When they see our actions, they will be drawn to talk to us. That will then open the door for us to speak truth and life into them. I know many times in my life before I knew the Lord I heard many people talking about how Jesus was our Savior and how awesome God was and that I needed to accept him. These same people were participating in the very sinful things that used to consume my life. . I saw others treating everyone around them like they were nothing and worthless. Many of those who told me about Jesus were obviously one person on Sunday and another the rest of the week. I can remember thinking, *What is so great about their God? He has not done anything special for them and they are no different than any one else, so why bother?* It got to a point that anytime someone would mention Jesus, an instant wall would go up and I would block out anything he or she had to say because as far as I was concerned, he or she was a hypocrite. After becoming a Christian, I have had people come up to me and ask me why I thought being a Christian meant anything. They would share with me the things they have seen other Christians doing.

This taught me it is extremely important as a

Christian to keep everything we do and say in check. If we don't, our witness will be of no effect and can actually hinder someone from coming to the Lord. We might try and excuse it away by saying, "Well, people have to understand we are all sinners and make mistakes. People have to understand that just because we go to church, it does not mean we are perfect. That is why God gives us grace and forgiveness." It is true; we all fall short and God does give us grace, but his grace is what enables us to do what is right. It might not be right to look at us to see God, but they don't know the truth yet. We do. Until they know the Lord for themselves, we are all they have to see him. If we don't stand apart, God does not look so hot to them.

You and I are how the world perceives God. We are ambassadors for Christ the Bible tells us in 2 Corinthians 5:20, "Now then we are ambassadors for Christ, as though God did beseech you by us: we pray you in Christ's stead, be ye reconciled to God." In Greek the word for ambassador is *presbeuo*. It means to be a senior, such as by implication, act as a representative and figuratively as a preacher. An ambassador represents someone or something else other than himself. As an ambassador, we are to act as a representative of Jesus Christ. This verse does not give us a choice. If we are Christians, then we are ambassadors. An ambassador is figuratively a preacher. So we are all called to preach and act as a representative to God's Word so that others might be reconciled to God. It is critical to think about how we are representing Christ. It is not enough to tell. We need to represent, and when we do that we are doing it in action. We are representing the King of kings. How are we making him look?

Jesus commanded us to go and tell the world about

him and to teach them to observe all that he commanded. "Go ye therefore, and teach all nations, baptizing them in the name of the Father, and of the Son, and of the Holy Ghost: Teaching them to observe all things whatsoever I have commanded you: and, lo, I am with you always, even unto the end of the world. Amen" (Matthew 28:19–20). The word *observe* is *tereo* and means to guard from loss or injury properly by keeping the eye upon. When you are keeping an eye on something or guarding it, you are totally focused on it. So we see Jesus saying to teach all to focus on all He has commanded. He also states that He will be with us the whole time. Jesus will be there to guide us and help us if we allow Him to. The Bible tells us in James 1:5, "If any of you lack wisdom, let him ask of God, that giveth to all men liberally, and upbraideth not; and it shall be given him."

The Bible has so much to tell us and is filled with many important things that give us direction for our life and insight into the heart of God. It is important for us to read the Bible so that we can truly know and understand the God we serve. We need to be striving to read though the entire Bible over time. I am not asking you to make a plan to read the entire Bible immediately. Make a reasonable goal to allow yourself to do this based on the amount of time you have and are able to read each day. For example, there are many Bibles and journals that give you a plan to read through the Bible in a year by reading three to five chapters a day. Only you and God know your capabilities, so if this is too much to start, try one or two chapters a day. This way you are taking two to five years. This is a long-term goal, not an immediate goal. I do want to encourage you to diligently strive to read God's entire Word over time. Do not get overwhelmed in doing so. Take one day at a time, reading more each day. It is impossible to do as He has commanded you and fully know and believe all that He says if you don't know for yourself all that He has to say. The more you know of His Word, the more you are able to grow and step into all that He has for you.

Father, I thank you and praise you for giving me your word. I thank you that you are always there and hear me. Lord, I pray that you would give me wisdom to discern your word. Lord, I pray that your discernment floods my mind that I might understand your Word and apply it in my life. Thank you, Lord, for giving me the ability to accomplish all that you have called me to do. I commit to pleasing you, Lord, rather than others. I submit to your will and judgments and repent for judging others. God, I choose to forgive those who have hurt me and remember their offense no more. Lord, please help me replace anger with your love. I love you, God, and thank you for all you have done and all that you will do.

You can use the space provided below to write down notes or thoughts about the chapter or prayer.

_____

_____

_____

_____

FAITH IN ACTION QUESTIONS

It is good to find a scripture that really means a lot to you and helps you get through the rough times. If you have a favorite scripture, write it below. If you don't, find one. Writing it out helps you remember it.

Scripture verse:

_____

_____

_____

_____

Remember, this verse is great to help encourage you, but it can't feed you for the rest of your life.

1. How much time every day do I spend in the Word?

_____

2. Do I tend to read the same things over and over?

_____

3. How much of the Bible have I read? How will I read more?

_____

_____

4. Has God asked me to do anything that I refused to do because it seemed impossible? What was it?

_____

_____

I choose now to let go of these thoughts that do not line up with the truth. I choose now to believe God is capable of the impossible. I turn every situation or task that is too big for me alone over to God. I will watch and see his glory manifested in my life.

5. Who have I allowed to be in charge of my life: me or God?

_____

6. Do I use God as a backup plan in case mine does not work out? Or make my own backup plan in case God's does not work out?

_____

7. What areas of my life do I need to relinquish control over and hand the reigns over to God?

_____

_____

_____

8. What are my motives when I do things?

_____

_____

9. Am I seeking the approval of men or God?

_____

10. Why?

_____

_____

11. Are there past issues in my life that could be driving this?

_____

12. What are they, and how can I resolve these feelings?

_____

Lord, I praise you for dying on the cross for me. I thank you, Lord, that you continually stand by me. I forgive myself and any others who have caused me pain and aided in my wrong motives. I seek your approval alone and I pray that you help me to see and walk the path that you have called me on, despite the opinions of others. I love you, Lord. Amen.

13. Can people tell I am a Christian and serve the Most High? Is my light shining? Or do I blend in well with the rest of the world?

_____

14. What have I done lately to show my light so that others can give God glory?

_____

15. What can I do to let my light shine?

_____

Remembered Promises and Forgotten Actions

> Behold, I set before you this day a blessing and a curse; A blessing, if ye obey the commandments of the LORD your God, which I command you this day: And a curse, if ye will not obey the commandments of the LORD your God, but turn aside out of the way which I command you this day, to go after other gods, which ye have not known.
>
> Deuteronomy 11:26–28

God is our heavenly Father, and he rewards us for good and obedient behavior to His Word. We are created in God's image and have some natural instincts to follow in His ways. It feels right. A father will reward his children when he is pleased with them. When we misbehave or we are not obedient as children, we are rebuked, corrected, and punished. When we are a parent, we do this because we love our children and want them to grow and become the best people they can be. God also wants us to grow spiritually so that we can be the best servant and child of God possible and complete and receive all that he has planned for us. God has given us this instinct with our children to show us his ways and heart. We can see how he works on a small scale so we can have an understanding on a big scale. God is, of course, much more powerful, and He never bends as we sometimes do. His Word is truth, and He is just. He loves you and all of his children. Just as we love our children no matter what they do, so does God. At times we might be disappointed and not approving of their behavior, yet we still love them. We love, discipline, and reward our children for the things they do and do not do. God does also. When we do as he says, we are rewarded. When we don't obey, sometimes He has to discipline if we will not listen and adhere to His rebuke. Yet no matter what, He loves us. Praise God!

We are responsible for the choices we make. No one can be to blame but ourselves. God has told us what will happen for the choices we make. We must choose the path of life and blessing. That path is Jesus and obedience to him.

Many Christians or people attending church today are continually told what God can do for them. In many cases they are not told what they must do to receive these promises from God. They soon become bitter at God, the preachers, pastors, and brothers and sisters in Christ because they have not received what they were told and were expecting. This may have even happened to you. God has so many things He wants to give us. There are many promises and blessings the Bible speaks of. They are all for each and every one of us, but they all come with a price. God expects things from us. There are things or actions we must do to receive them. The Bible tells us do this and we will be blessed with that. The Bible is loaded with examples, both in the Old and

New Testament. It is up to us to seek them out, pull them apart, and really study them. Look up definitions in a dictionary and look up the original Greek and Hebrew words and the meanings of them. It can really help to bring clarity along with embedding His instruction into your heart. When it becomes embedded in your heart, it will become a natural process for you to do these things. You will truly get a deeper love and reverent understanding of the fear of the Lord, which is the beginning of knowledge (Proverbs 1:7). In the end you will be blessed at your every move. Notice in the scriptures that follow, I have italicized the action part of the scripture.

Doing what the Lord has commanded has many rewards and benefits. Proverbs lists a benefit that many people need. Many people struggle with a life of fear of what bad things might happen. The awesome thing is no one has to! God tells us the way out in Proverbs 1:33: "But *whoso hearkeneth unto me* shall dwell safely, and shall be quiet from fear of evil." *Hearkeneth* means to listen and obey. When we do this, it is our insurance of safety. If we are doing what God has told us, there is absolutely nothing to fear. God is far superior and mightier than the devil. Fear and faith can't coexist, so choose faith and all fear will disappear.

> *My son, if thou wilt receive my words, and hide my commandments with thee; So that thou incline thine ear unto wisdom, and apply thine heart to understanding; Yea, if thou criest after knowledge, and liftest up thy voice for understanding; If thou seekest her as silver, and searchest for her as for hid treasures;* Then shalt thou understand the fear of the LORD, and find the knowledge of God.
> Proverbs 2:1–5

It is amazing how many people pay big bucks trying to get longer life. People pay for pills, herbs, natural remedies, and for many treatments from doctors to prolong life. Scientists have spent lifetimes making things trying to give us a longer life. Corporations invest a lot of money to fund this research. God tells us that if we keep his commands, our days will be prolonged in Deuteronomy 6:2: "*That thou mightest fear the Lord thy God, to keep all his statues and commandments, which I command thee, thou, and thy son, and thy son's son, all the days of thy life;* and that thy days may be prolonged." God has had the answer right in front of us the whole time. Everyone wants and seeks ways to get peace. Many people try all sorts of relaxation techniques to feel at peace. God tells us the way to get it in Romans 8:6: "For to be carnally minded is death; *but to be spiritually minded* is life and peace." Proverbs 3:1–2 tells how to receive both long life and peace "My son, *forget not my law; but let thine heart keep my commandments*: for length of days, and long life, and peace shall they add to thee." All of these scriptures clearly show us that we need to stop looking to man and worldly ways to live longer and receive peace and instead turn to God and what He has said and we will have them both for free.

We need to be thirsty for the Lord and the living water that He gives us. When we allow our thirst for Him consume us, we will overcome all our fleshly desires and things of this world and begin to be filled with an overflow of living water that pours out of us and splashes onto all those around us and those we come in contact with. When we overcome the things of this world, we will inherit all things! Revelation 21:6–7 reminds us of this: "And he said unto me, It is done. I am Alpha and Omega, the beginning and the end. I will give unto him *that is athirst* of the fountain of the water of life freely. *He that overcometh* shall inherit all things; and I will be his God, and he shall be my son." When we are athirst (thirsty) for something we feel as though nothing else will satisfy us and we will take extreme actions to get it. Jesus's blood that He shed for us is the fountain. The word *fountain* in this text is the Greek word *pege* and is translated in Strong's as "source or supply (of water, blood, enjoyment) (not necessarily the original spring)." Jesus is our source of shed blood and living water. The water the Lord Gives us turns into everlasting life (John 4:14). We need to be thirsty for the Lord and what He has done and then we will be given what we desire and be satisfied and be given all we need to overcome and receive all things that the Lord has for us.

God will shield you from things that attack you, but you have to trust him. The Bible states in Proverbs 30:5, "Every word of God is pure: he is a shield unto them *that put their trust in him.*" When we trust the Lord, we are allowing Him to protect us and shield us. Without trust in the Lord, we leave ourselves wide open. The choice is ours. It is not up to God to automatically protect us; it is up to us to make the choice to trust in Him. After that the shield is automatic. God gives us free will; we must take action to receive. When you trust, you are not fearful. Fear and trust can't coexist. When you know in your head what God has said, yet doubt in your heart that he will do it for you, it is being double minded. Be sure and know with everything inside of you no matter what things look like, God *will* take care of you.

God longs for and commands us to return to Him when we backslide in Jeremiah 3:14–15: "*Turn, O backsliding chil*dren, saith the Lord; For I am married unto you: and I will take one of a city, and two of a family, and I will bring you to Zion: And I will give you pastors according to my heart, which shall feed you with knowledge and understanding." God says if you are returning to your old way of life and no longer following him and you turn back to him, he will give you pastors who will give you the spiritual food you need to gain knowledge and understanding. If we have these things, it makes life much easier to walk through. Pastors truly are a blessing from the Lord. Take note that the Lord says the pastor will be according to His heart, not ours, so we need be sure to stay where He has placed us. There is a reason for where we are placed and who is placed over us.

"And Jesus said unto them, *Because of your unbelief*: for verily I say unto you, *If ye have faith as a grain of mustard seed*, ye shall say unto this mountain, Remove hence to yonder place; and it shall remove; and nothing shall be impossible unto you" (Matthew 17:20). Remember from chapter one that the word unbelief in Greek means unfaithfulness (disobedience). So Jesus states here that the apostles were unable to perform certain things because of unbelief (disobedience). The word *mountain* is translated in the Greek as "to rise or rear." When we have faith, belief, and trust in and loyalty to God, he will remove the obstacle rising up in your way. He has given us the authority and power to speak to our problems and obstacles, and they will have to move from out of our way. There is just one key action: have faith. Believe (be obedient) and they will go away; do not doubt in your heart or fear them.

In Matthew 5:1, Jesus went and sat on a hill after seeing the people. He then spoke the words in Matthew 5:3–11: "Blessed are the *poor in spirit*: for theirs is the kingdom of heaven. Blessed are they that *mourn*: for they shall be comforted. Blessed are the *meek*: for they shall inherit the earth. Blessed are they which do *hunger and thirst after righteousness*: for they shall be filled. Blessed are the *merciful*: for they shall obtain mercy. Blessed are the *pure in heart*: for they shall see God. Blessed are the *peacemakers*: for they shall be called the children of God. Blessed are they which are *persecuted for righteousness' sake*: for theirs is the kingdom of heaven. Blessed are ye, when men shall revile you, and persecute you, and shall say all manner of evil against you falsely, for my sake (italics added)." We know that whatever Jesus speaks comes straight from the throne of God, because He only speaks what His father in heaven tells Him (John 12:49–50, John 14:24). The one that sticks out to me the most here is when it states we are blessed when we hunger and thirst after righteousness. When we hunger and thirst, we are driven to be filled. The thought of eating or drinking consumes our thoughts. It is hard to concentrate or focus on anything else until we have been filled. If our hunger and thirst are for the things of God, then we will be blessed. Many of these traits are of a humble person who is diligently seeking to please the Lord and be obedient. These are all pretty straightforward. God will bless you if you do these things. These are all traits that we should be striving toward; some are easier for us than others, yet the closer we get to God, the easier they become, because the closer we get to God, the closer He gets to us. The more of God is in us, His traits become ours, and we are able to do these things naturally.

If you are walking in an appointment set forth by God and loving him—obeying—everything will work out for good even if it does not appear that way for the moment. In Romans 8:28, it states, "And we know that all things work together for good to them that love God, to them that are called according to his purpose." When we continue steadfastly in God's will for us and don't pay attention to all the negative happenings in life and keep our eyes focused on Him knowing that He is using every circumstance in our life to grow us and mold us, everything will work out for the best. God uses everything to help us grow into a better person and step into the plan that He has for each and every one of us. Although we can't always see this as we are walking through the circumstance, it usually becomes clear at a later date. Everything leads to an outcome that we can't fully know, yet God does. Many of us try to use this scripture to comfort others, unbelievers, in their time of crisis. We need to be careful; it should be explained that it could work out for good if they choose to love and follow God because this scripture clearly states that this will be if we love God. When we love God, we follow Him and His ways. We don't want to be misquoting God and leaving out important actions needed from us to receive what God has. When we only quote half the scripture to unbelievers, we are robbing them of the truth by only telling them half of it. It might seem hard to share the whole truth, but we don't know what God has planned. This moment could be a turning point for them and an amazing testimony. Even if the person we are sharing this with doesn't choose to act on it now, he will never forget the truth spoken to him, and it will minister to him at a later date.

Life can be hard at times; we all have struggles and trials that we walk through in life. At times it can feel like no matter how hard we try to do what is right, we still can't get ahead. This is a lie that the devil keeps telling us to stop us from doing what God has called us to do and to stop us from reaping the harvest that God has ordained in due season. Galatians 6:9 reminds us of this: "And *let us not be weary in well doing*: for in due season we shall reap, *if we faint not* (italics added)." If we don't get bitter, tired, and eventually give up in doing what is right, then in God's (not ours) perfect timing, we will get a harvest from the Lord. To receive what he has for us, we can't give up. We usually receive a breakthrough right after things have been the toughest.

Decide to be a servant of the Lord, do what he says, and resist (meaning to stand against or oppose) the devil, and then the devil *will* go away. That is what God says will happen in James 4:7: "*Submit* yourselves therefore to God. *Resist the devil*, and He will flee from you. *Draw nigh to God*, and he will draw nigh to you. *Cleanse your hands, ye sinners; and purify your hearts, ye double minded* (italics added)." To be double minded is to say one thing yet think or act another way. For example, you say you trust God to take care of something or to fulfill a word of prophecy in your life, yet you are making a backup plan for yourself just in case He does not come through when you think he should. Trust that God will show Himself mighty. We have a tendency to wait for God to show up and get close to us before we take action. We have this mind-set that God is supposed to take the first step, and then when we feel him, we will step in closer to Him. In reality, God is saying, "Move into me, get close to me, and then I will move closer to you." Take the first step, the step of faith.

God tells us to ask and we will receive at the beginning of Mathew 7:7: "*Ask*, and it shall be given you; *seek*, and ye shall find; *knock*, and it shall be opened unto you: For every one that *asketh* receiveth; and he that *seeketh* findeth; and to him that *knocketh* it shall be opened (italics added)." Many Christians take this to mean that God will give us whatever we want and that God is somehow subject to us and what we demand of him. Even if we or others don't say it or say that this statement is not how they feel, they are double minded because their actions and expectations of God prove otherwise. We need to stop and seriously check our heart in this matter. We are subject to God! He is not subject to us. We can see in James 4:3 that we are to submit to God. "Ye ask, and receive not, because ye ask amiss, that ye may consume it upon your lusts." James clears this up when he states when we don't get what we are asking for it is because we are asking for it outside of God's will. Instead we are asking for it out of our own fleshly desires and wants for everything, thinking we need the best of everything and we need it now. Seek God, His wisdom, knowledge, and will for your life and you will find it. Knock and any door that might be concealing the answer and God will open it. Search God out and you will discover more than you ever imagined and find true joy.

It is important that we are doing these things for the right motives. If we are only doing the things God says to get the blessing, we will not likely receive the blessing. We need to be doing the things he has commanded because we love and honor him. Then the blessings will follow. If we act out of pure greed, it is the same as asking amiss. Obey God and keep his commands because you love him and are thankful for what he has done for you. It is important to remember that God gives us commands and then tells us what we will receive for our obedience. We need to get off the mind-set of praying for God to bless us and focusing all of our attention on the blessing. Instead we need to be focusing on being obedient to God, praising Him for making the ultimate sacrifice and dying on the cross to take the punishment for our sin, and seeking his will for us. We don't even have to worry about it. When we are obedient, the blessings are automatic! God says he will do it and he will. So focus on God and do what He says and let others marvel at the blessings that follow you.

> Lord, I acknowledge your divine wisdom and power. I magnify you, for you truly hold the world in the palm of your hand. The more I search you out, learn about you, and come into the obedience of your Word, the more awe-inspiring you become. Though I may never fully understand you until I get to heaven and am standing in your presence, I will continue to get closer to you by knowing you all the days of my life. I thank you that you have given me your Word to help me walk out in righteousness the life you have given me. I pray that as I study your Word you give me fresh revelation and understanding that I might better serve you. I love you, Lord. Amen.

You can use the space provided below to write down notes or thoughts about the chapter or prayer.

_____

_____

_____

_____

FAITH IN ACTION QUESTIONS

1. Have I been expecting a promise or blessing from God?

_____

2. What is it?

_____

_____

3. What does God require from me for him to meet this promise or blessing?

_____

_____

_____

4. Have I met his requirements for him to fulfill this promise?

_____

5. What are my motives?

_____

6. Have I focused all my attention on receiving the blessing instead of focusing on God?

_____

7. What will I do with the blessing the Lord gives me?

_____

8. Am I being double minded, making up backup plans? If so, what are they?

_____

_____

_____

I choose to release them now and wait expectantly on the Lord.

9. Am I open to receiving a rebuke or correction from the Lord, or do I get mad and refuse to acknowledge my faults?

_____

10. Am I choosing to walk in the fear of the Lord to gain knowledge and not be a fool as Proverbs 1:7 tells me?

_____

11. Am I walking in a curse because of disobedience? If so, what am I going to do about it?

_____

_____

_____

HEARING AND OBEYING THE VOICE OF THE LORD

The Lord wants his blessings to overtake us. He makes this very clear in Deuteronomy 28:2: "And all these blessings shall come on thee, and overtake thee, if thou shalt hearken unto the voice of the Lord thy God." The key to this is to hearken unto his voice. The Hebrew word for *hearken* is *shama*. Strong's Concordance defines it as "a primitive root; to hear intelligently often with implication of attention, obedience, etc.; causatively, to tell, etc." So when we are hearkening to the Lord, we are hearing him intelligently with obedience. One way to intelligently listen to and obey God is to read and obey his written Word: the Bible. There is another way to hear from the Lord that is also extremely important. Deuteronomy 28:2 speaks of this: listening intelligently with obedience to his voice. We need to take time to be listening for the Lord.

The Lord recently spoke to me as I was at home worshiping him and praying. He gave me a word and told me it was for the church. I remember thinking as He gave it to me that it was quite a bit longer than the usual word he gives me to bring to church, but I was obedient to give it the following Sunday with the permission of my pastor. After church we had an altar call. One woman had come up for prayer; after ministering to her, we were talking, and she looked at me and told me I should write the word the Lord had given me down and hand it out to others who were not there at the church that Sunday. Later on that day we were having a cookout at our home to celebrate the baptism of my children. Some family and people from my church had come. I was talking with one of my close friends from church who had discipled me as a young Christian; she told me that I should write the word the Lord had given me down and hand it out to people who were not there. The following day, I received the call from Tate's Publishing telling me that they wanted to publish my book. As I was editing this book for publication, the Lord clearly showed me that the word he had spoken to my heart a couple weeks earlier needed to be spoken or written to all Christians, not only to my church. It was as he had spoken, "for the church"—his church, the entire church. So here is the last part of what the Lord spoke to my heart to share with you, the church.

It is time to take a stand and be unmovable. It is time to draw on the Lord's strength and quit trying to draw on your own. The Lord has many things for you to do. You will need His strength. Stop living two lives. Follow Him and His ways and see the gates of heaven flung open wide. Seek Him, His will, and His ways. He is the One True God. He is your Savior, your Strength, your Peace, your Joy, and your Master. Submit to His Authority and experience true freedom and peace. His children know His voice and follow it. If you have not heard the voice of your Lord, today is your day. Focus on Him. Let all the cares of this world pass away, call on Him, and wait for Him.

It is crucial in this time that you hear and recognize the voice of your Master and Lord. Knowing the voice of your Lord removes all doubt and uncertainty. Knowing His voice will stop attacks that come and speak to you and try and draw you away from the truth. When you hear the voice of your Lord you are able to receive His correction and guidance. Without it you are left to try and find your way in the dark. You all need to be secure in your own faith. It is not a time to lean on the faith of others to be fed. It is time to build your own faith and relationship with Him. You can't live and draw off the relationship that others have with Him. The time of milk is over. It is time for your sustenance. Children, it is time to get off the bottle. It is time to grow and eat solid food. He is weaning you. Throw down the bottle and pick up a steak.

This is a key step in your walk with Him. This is a key to the rest of your life and ministry that He is calling you to. Before you let that thought creep into your head that says "I am not called to ministry and I don't want to be," let Him tell you through His written Word and still, small voice (the Holy Spirit) that each and every one of you, if you are a follower of His, is called to ministry. Your life and the way you live it is a ministry. The example to those around you and your family is a ministry.

Today is your day! This is a stepping stone, a building block, and a key to open a door for you. Do not let it pass you by! He has more than crumbs for you. Do you think that you are not worthy or spiritual enough to hear your heavenly Father? That is a lie straight out of the pit of hell. No one was good enough, that is why Jesus died on the cross, so that you would all have salvation. He is the Father of all. He does not love your pastor, your parents, your neighbor, or anyone else more than He loves you. He loves you just as much as anyone else. Jesus died for you. He was sent for you. God longs to commune with you. He wants and does speak with you and I. You only need to listen. Today is your day to receive it. Today is your day to hear from your Father.

When the things of this world come to tempt you, turn to God and his Word. Jesus himself said man (we) can't live by bread (the things of this world, things of the flesh) alone, but we need the words of God to truly live. When you live to hear the Lord, then you are truly living. Otherwise, you are merely surviving. Have you seen the show *Survivor*? The people on there are alive, but they are miserable. They have to fight and struggle through much just to get by. Is that how you want to be, pushing and struggling and fighting to just barely survive? Or do you want to truly live your life? Do you want to survive or live?

I know the Lord can speak to you. No matter what you have done or what you have been through. If God will speak to me, He will speak to anyone. Before knowing the Lord, I was an alcoholic and a drug addict; I practiced witchcraft and fornication. I was a liar, a thief, and much more. I still make mistakes in my walk with him, but through His grace, His Word, and voice, he leads me back on the right path. God can and does speak to you. You just have to take the time to listen.

The main thing in hearing the voice of the Lord that I think most people miss is when you talk to the Lord, you need to pause. Take the time to focus on Him and wait for Him to talk back. A conversation is two-way. Stop thinking about everything else that you have to or want to do. Clear your mind and meditate on the Most High. Worship Him and praise Him.

You don't have to do all the talking in prayer. The more you listen for Him, the more you will hear from Him. The more you hear from Him, the easier it becomes to recognize His voice. It is okay to receive words of knowledge and prophecy from others, just don't rely on them. Rely on God. Most of the time, words from others can act as a confirmation and a confidence builder in what the Lord has already shown or spoken to you. God uses all of us to build one another up and strengthen one another. He has placed each of us strategically where He wants us so we can work together. He does not want us seeking others for our faith; He wants us seeking Him, so let today be the first day of your long and wonderful walk with him.

So rejoice! The Lord of all creation wants to commune with you. He says today is your day! Don't let it pass you by.

> Thank you, Lord, that you sent your Son, Jesus, for me and that He is alive today. Thank you that you want to speak to me and guide me in my life. I choose to believe in you and be obedient to your Word and voice. Help me to get rid of the business of my mind so that I might hear from you. I choose to cast all thoughts that are not from you out of my mind. I will believe the truth and not the lie. In Jesus's holy name, I ask. Amen.

You can use the space provided below to write down notes or thoughts about the chapter or prayer.

_____

_____

_____

Faith in Action Questions

1. Have I heard the voice of the Lord?

_____

2. Do I take time to listen for the Lord?

_____

3. Would I obey if he told me to do something?

_____

4. When can I make time to listen?

_____

5. Do I listen to and obey every voice I hear?

_____

6. Do I make sure what I hear lines up with the Word of God?

_____

7. Do I choose to cast out of my mind anything that exalts itself over the Word of God?

_____

8. What lies have I believed?

_____

_____

9. What is the truth to replace that lie?

_____

_____

10. What action can I take to get rid of distractions around me and in my mind while I am focusing on the Lord?

_____

_____

EPILOGUE

Our journey as Christians never ends until we have left this earthly body and are reunited with God. It does not even truly end there; it is just another chapter for us in eternity. So do not let this end your process of refining yourself. We are to always be self-examining our lives. This will stop us from allowing open doors in our life for the enemy. It is good to keep yourself in check. Let us look at the log in our own eyes before taking the speck out of others. We need to be in constant forgiveness of ourselves and to all those around us so that we might receive the forgiveness of the Father. Let us remember to speak life into our own lives and into the lives of all God's children around us.

May God continue to pour out his blessing upon you. May you continue to walk in his anointing, authority, and will. May you receive favor wherever you go. May the Lord of all creation bless all that you put your hand to do for Him. May you continue to grow in wisdom and understanding. May the Lord Almighty give you discernment and revelation as you continue to seek Him out and grow closer to Him. May His voice be crystal clear in your ear. May the Lord bless your life and the lives of all those in whom you come in contact with.

May your light so shine before men that they give your Father in heaven glory. Amen.

GLOSSARY

Abominable, (Greek) *bdeluktos*: detestable

Ambassador, (Greek) *presbeuo*: senior, i.e., (by implication) act as a representative (figuratively, preacher)

Believe: to have a firm persuasion of any thing; to expect or hope with confidence; to trust

Circumspectly: (Greek) *akribos; exactly*

Cleave: (Hebrew) *dabaq*; to impinge, i.e., cling or adhere; figuratively, to catch by pursuit

Comply: to conform or adapt one's actions to another's wishes, to a rule, or to necessity

Devotion: a religious exercise or practice other than the regular corporate worship of a congregation

Faith: belief, or the object of belief; the substance *(realization)* of things hoped for, the evidence *(conviction)* of things not seen

Hate, (Greek) *miseo*: to detest (especially to persecute); by extension, to love less

Hearkeneth, (Hebrew) *shama*: to hear intelligently (often with implication of attention, obedience, etc.; causatively, to tell, etc.)

Hope: devotion to Christ produced a religious experience that gave certainty to hope

Hypocrisy, (Greek) *prosecho*: also translated as to have regard

Justified, (Greek) *dikaioo*: to render (i.e., show or regard as) just or innocent

Lord, (Greek) *kurios*: from *kuros* (supremacy); supreme in authority, i.e. (as noun) controller; by implication, Master (as a respectful title)

Manifest, (Greek) *phaneroo*: to make apparent

Mountain, (Greek) *oros*: to rise or rear

Observe, (Greek) *tereo*: to guard from loss or injury, properly, by keeping the eye upon Religious: relating to or manifesting faithful devotion to an acknowledged ultimate reality or deity; a religious person; religious attitudes

Render, (Greek) *apodidomi*: to give away, i.e., up, over, back, etc.

Reprobate, (Greek) *adokimos*: from *adoki*, not
acknowledged. Not genuine can be simply
attached to the word; to refuse to accept; reject
(transitive verb) rejected as worthless or not
standing a test: condemned (adjective)

Seared, (Greek) *kausteriazo*; to brand ("cauterize"), i.e.,
(by implication) to render unsensitive (figuratively)
Serve: to be a servant to, attend; to give the
service and respect due to (a superior); to
comply with the commands or demands of

Profit, (Greek) *ofeleo* to be useful, i.e., to benefit

Unbelief, (Greek) *apistia*, unfaithfulness (disobedience)

Vain, (Greek) *kenos*: empty (literally or figuratively)

BIBLIOGRAPHY

http://dictionary.crossmap.com/letter/p.htm
   Encyclopedia Britannica Dictionary
   (Encyclopedia Britannica Inc., 2005)

Encyclopedia Britannica Student Library
   CD version 2005 CD-ROM

King James Dictionary
   http://av1611.com/kjbp/kjv-dictionary.html

Revised International Standard Bible Encyclopedia
   (International Bible Translators, Inc., 1997)
   Theophilos 3, Ivan Jurik., 1997–2004, CD-ROM

Revised Strong's Hebrew–Aramaic Dictionary
   (International Bible Translators, Inc., 1999)
   Theophilos 3, Ivan Jurik., 1997–2004, CD-ROM

Revised Strong's Greek Dictionary
   (International Bible Translators, Inc., 1999)
   Theophilos 3, Ivan Jurik., 1997–2004, CD-ROM

United States Life expectancy
   http://en.wikipedia.org/wiki/List_of_countries_
   by_life_expectancy